# Lectures and Orations by Henry Ward Beecher

# Lectures and Orations
## By Henry Ward Beecher

*Edited by*
### NEWELL DWIGHT HILLIS

**AMS PRESS, INC.**
NEW YORK

Reprinted from the edition of 1913, New York
First AMS EDITION published 1970
Manufactured in the United States of America


International Standard Book Number: 0-404-00699-X


Library of Congress Catalog Card Number: 72-126662



AMS PRESS, INC.
NEW YORK, N.Y. 10003

# Contents

# Foreword

FOR more than forty years Henry Ward Beecher was one of the two or three most conspicuous figures in American life. During all these years he divided honours with the man who happened to be President and the occasional banker, inventor, author or statesman who for the hour stood in the limelight. More men heard Mr. Beecher preach and lecture than any other American speaker. More people read what Mr. Beecher wrote than any other writer. More people knew Mr. Beecher than any other man upon our streets or cars. He left behind more than forty volumes, including sermons, patriotic addresses, essays, theology, philosophy, with studies of travel, nature and art. He was successful as preacher, lecturer, editor, essayist, and statesman. Not once in a thousand years does a man appear in the world of whom we can say as was said of Theseus, " Whether he ran, or whether he walked, or whether he stood, he conquered."

Popularity is like the tides of the sea ; it

rises and falls. The influence of a truly good and great man is like the mountains and the stars; it stands fast forever. From his youth the pilgrim host looked to Henry Ward Beecher as to the Moses who was to lead them out of the wilderness into the promised land. Multitudes of our people never made up their minds on any great question of religion, politics or social reform, until first of all they had taken their bearings from Beecher's thinking. All this is the more wonderful when we remember that Beecher never had the assistance of high office. Grant's arm was strengthened by the might of a half million men standing behind him. The office of the Presidency lent weight to Lincoln's words. The history of the Republic holds the names of at least ten Presidents who through some compromise or happy accident were elevated to the White House. But yesterday this private citizen was not able to make his voice heard far beyond the limits of his own town; to-day as President this same man's voice may ring to the borders of the Rio Grande and the Oregon. But by sheer weight of personal manhood Beecher maintained an influence as great as that exerted by other men as senators or Presidents.

# Foreword

Among the secrets of the power of Henry Ward Beecher we shall find one in his splendid body and marvellous health. He was, perhaps, the finest animal and the best illustration of a perfect body as the instrument of fine thinking afforded by his generation. From his fathers also he had the gift of unique common sense that made him reasonable, fair, and sane. He had the rare gift of intellectual sympathy, so that instinctively he put himself in the other man's place. He was our Nineteenth Century illustration also of John Bunyan's Great-Heart, using his genius as a shield above the weak and oppressed. He had the most extraordinary gift of language, choosing words with a certain exquisite sense of the inevitable. He had reverence for the truth, justice towards men, love towards God; he had moral earnestness, wit, humour, gentleness, courage,—and by his combination of gifts he captured the admiration of the American people. It is not too much to say that Beecher changed the thinking of our people as to their idea of God, the Bible, and the genius of Christianity. He was the first man to take the sting out of the early theories of Evolution, and who found in science a real aid to religion. Indeed, the very atmosphere

# Foreword

of the churches of our land has been different because Henry Ward Beecher lived and wrought.

At a critical hour during the Civil War, Henry Ward Beecher pleaded the cause of the Republic before the English people. Some time during the autumn of 1863, England practically entered into a compact with France to recognize the Southern Confederacy on January 1, 1864. Two influences brought this about. On the one hand, the English patrician, loving the throne and the monarchy, wished the Republic to go to pieces. On the other hand, the English cotton spinners, after two years of starvation because no raw cotton could be obtained from the South, had become desperate, driven to crusts, rags and idleness. Although they manfully endured their distresses, believing in the cause of free labour, their condition lent excuse to the British governing class for favouring the South. Beecher was abroad in the interest of his health and at the charges of Plymouth Church. He had no commission from Abraham Lincoln or his country. Believing that the recognition of the South by England and France might be fatal to the Union, Beecher gave a series of five addresses, beginning in Manchester and

# Foreword

ending in Exeter Hall, London. William Taylor went away after Beecher's address in Liverpool to say, "No such eloquence has been heard in the world since Demosthenes pleaded the cause of Athens against King Philip." After reading those speeches Abraham Lincoln told his cabinet that if the war was ever fought to a successful issue, there would be but one man to lift the flag at Fort Sumter, for without Beecher in England there might have been no flag to raise.

The later years of Beecher's life brought other crises to his country. In the name of patriotism and education, family life and social reform, he delivered many orations and lectures. In the interest of multitudes who never had an opportunity of seeing such transient reports of them as may have been accessible at the time, some of these addresses of the great preacher have been brought together in this more permanent form.

NEWELL DWIGHT HILLIS.

The oration on Lincoln is given as reported in Beecher's "Patriotic Addresses in America and England, 1850-1876," by permission of Mr. Wm. C. Beecher, as representative of the owners of the copyright. That book offers, in the great orator's own words, the most complete view of his political career.

# I

## PURITANISM [1]

IN one of the mightiest battles of the Spanish Peninsula, Napier, I think it is, who records that a truce was sounded at noon, that the war of artillery ceased, the smoke cleared away, and the men, who but an hour before had been whirling like storms upon each other in headlong charges, came down to a brook which divided the ground, to quench their thirst, and reached forth friendly hands and exchanged kind greetings across it. To-night, ladies and gentlemen, there is a truce around the Plymouth Rock. We seize this charmed hour to hush every conflict, to let the whirl of business run out to stillness, to quench the fires of party. The most earnest men will pause to-night, and from opposite sides look kindly at each other. We reach hands across the Plymouth Stone, and greet each other. Peace be with you! To be sure it is the eve

[1] Delivered first in Philadelphia, December 21, 1860, before the New England Society, and substantially repeated often as a lecture.

of the 22d, but let us gently abolish twelve hours, and decree this to be the ever-memorable date of New England!

Even in Old England there are those who mark the 22d of December, for the children of the Pilgrims are not all upon this side of the ocean. As the sun leaves those shores and wheels hitherward, every hour awakes in ranks the States that celebrate that memorable date. Where there is a drop of New England blood there will be holy thoughts and grateful memories to-night—and where is there not New England blood? Is there a State of the glorious thirty-three that is unenriched by it? Her ingenious mechanics work in every nook upon the Continent. Her gentle schoolmistresses brood in schools along every league from Lake to Gulf—or, exalted to a higher sphere, preside over their own school, where husband is assistant usher, and children pupils. When a railroad needs method, when a bank needs keen sagacity, when iron or stone, wood or clay, are to be moulded, or water called from waste to usefulness, or steam subdued to industry—there you shall find the universal Yankee. Prolific stock! Wonderful hive! New England swarms forever, but it never runs empty. And no man born in New England ever forgets his mother, though her breast was granite, and her kiss frost.

To-night, then, in every State of this Union, there will be a time for grateful retrospection. Maine, amid her snows, will rehearse the story that never wears out by telling. New Hampshire, from amid her hills and mountains, will send back a grateful remembrance to the past, and an " All hail!" to the future. Vermont, her green hills now tucked up in white for their winter's sleep, will recount to her children the story of the wintry day and the welcomeless landing. Connecticut, small but comely, and Rhode Island, smaller but yet fair, shall stop all their machineries, and bare the head in the sacred memories of this hour. Let Massachusetts lead this throng, to whose shores came the Pilgrims. She guards the Rock, and a hundred tongues to-night eloquently speak its meaning.

Metropolitan New York admits to her calendar of saints as many as the world can find, so that they do not come dry-lipped; and while in due sequence she spreads a wondrous cheer on hospitable tables for the Knickerbocker and for the Gaul, for Santa Claus, for St. George and St. Patrick—thirsty saints all— and for St. Burns, elected to the saintship by

a thirst equal to any, she hails the coming of
the Pilgrim, mumbles her parched corn, con-
scientiously sips the water fervid with ices, re-
warding afterwards her exemplary temperance
with fare that would have appalled a Puritan,
albeit he was a man not averse to generous
diet.

So long as the trailing arbutus—true Mayflower—grows upon the hills of New Jersey,
she shall yield a welcome to this day ; for many
of her noblest cradles to-night rock the blood
of the Puritan.   And the great heart of Pennsylvania, to-night, true to its generous im-
pulses, and confessing how many that she loves
and honours come from the Puritan land—
opens to hail and bless the memory of the Pilgrims.   Delaware and Maryland, States that,
by the side of their neighbours, seem like punc-
tuation points, or particles, in the sentence that
spells Union and Liberty—not disjunctive particles, but inseparable conjunctions, binding
together the glorious eloquence of confederated
States !   And Virginia, what shall she say, to-
night ?   Uncover the head !   Draw near with
me, that I may ask—not those who forget, but
those who remember Washington.   Hark !
To-night Mount Vernon sends a greeting of
holy reverence to Plymouth Rock !   And

sweeping westward, every State—Ohio and Kentucky, Michigan and Indiana, Illinois and Missouri, Tennessee and Wisconsin, Iowa and Kansas—shall send patriotic thoughts to the ancestral shrine, for every one of them has New England blood! Yea, across the plains, along the mountain slope, in the cabins of the wearied miner, all down the coasts of California and Oregon, there shall be a grateful recognition of the Pilgrim Fathers, and from the gigantic evergreens of Calaveras goes a greeting to the pine trees of all New England.

Nor shall the wide compact of remembrance lose one State along the Gulf to-night—they shall drop the hand and cool the tongue, and from a thousand spots truce shall sound, and men come down to this peaceful memory that flows between us and exchange greetings.

By the God of the Pilgrims, I say to the North, give up; to the South, keep not back, but bring my sons from afar and my daughters from the ends of the earth, and reverence the memory of the Pilgrims! Let the Savannah murmur it; let the Mississippi sound it; let the Chesapeake and Delaware bear the chorus to the sea; then let the Atlantic speak and the Pacific answer—deep calling unto deep.

Two hundred and forty years ago! Who

will journey with me back to that period? Of how much must we divest ourselves before we can draw near to that eventful day, when the sea washed upon the shores of Plymouth the seed of states? You may not carry with you the vision of fruitful valleys—of populous cities, of fields of grain and grass. Restore if you can, in imagination, the solitude of the Continent! Put a few Spaniards in Florida, a few Englishmen at Jamestown, a few stragglers in Canada. Give back the whole continent to the Aboriginal Indian. Light his fire along the streams, and mark his hunting path again along the slopes of the Alleghany! Put out every lighthouse upon the coast, stop every mill, burn every ship. Nay, if you would be real pilgrims, in search of the Primitive Pilgrims, you must abolish the annals of history, cover up the battle-fields of the Revolution, the Yorktown, the Bunker Hill, the Camp at Valley Forge. You must plant the forest where your noble Continental State House now is, and silence that bell now consecrated to Liberty, but which then lay undug in the ores of the earth. You must roll back the tide of civilization, efface every railway, fill every canal, annihilate the steam engine, give back the telegraph wire to its

16

mine, and its subtle fluid to the vagrant stormy clouds, restore to science all those secrets of chemistry which now enrich the manufactories of the world; restore to nature the secrets of fertility; go back to the plough and implements of the olden time, and let steam ploughs and reapers retreat to their old hiding-places; destroy natural pity, and let birds fly back to unknown haunts, fish sink into the deep again, and the astronomer forget his way, and his path be rubbed out. Sink your yachts, obliterate your main and river steamers, scuttle your merchantmen and bird-rivalling clippers, and stand to see the ill-looking, clumsy *Mayflower* enter the harbour, a very tub which a Delaware lighterman would scorn.

Thus, divesting the imagination of the facts of the age in which we live, walk back to our fathers without seeing a schoolhouse or a church in all the way; without hearing a mill, or the lowing of the kine; without one verdant meadow for the scythe, or blossoming field for the bees; without an inn and without a host, without a road and without steed or carriage; without a companion save the Indian, and without a paper to print your observations, or a book to record your travels! In short, they who would see Plymouth Rock to-night as they saw it who landed two hundred and forty years ago, must disrobe the continent and strip bare the age in which he lives of its discoveries, inventions and accumulations of knowledge! And thus unapparelled see these men!

But they, too, must not stand forth in those pictures which the imagination loves to draw, full of colours, full of symmetries, full of grand heroic traits! They were men of like passions with ourselves. Some were heroes and some only heroic. Heroes never march in battalions! They were beset with ignorance which later ages have cleared away. They were narrow where we have grown broad. They were intolerant where we have grown liberal. They were rude and hard, while we have clad ourselves with a few graces. A grim and firm-faced band of men were they, who for liberty of conscience forsook home, and stood firm, on a December day upon the winter-locked shore of Plymouth, without a regret. How many of us, with all our boasted advances, could have stood on that Rock, blossoming only with frost-flowers, with old England behind and a howling wilderness before, and cast no look backwards, but like them, smile upon a welcome winter wilderness in which there was liberty! As sometimes, in a doubtful battle, a bold commander casts forward his flag among the enemy, that his followers, with new redoubled ardour, may strike forward to retake it there—so our fathers cast forward their hearts upon the wilderness, and it would be gloriously well if the sons could find indeed the heart of the fathers!

But it is time that we should look to these men, not in their peaked hats and slashed doublets, not in their clumsy cloaks and antique costumes, but in the habiliments of their souls! Let us compare these men of two hundred and forty years ago with their own age, and that age with our own!

There seem to be long winters in history as well as nature, out of which spring suddenly leaps; whose growth, slowly preparing through many months, is almost like enchantment. To-day snows, and to-morrow blossoms. Certain it was that despotism, civil and ecclesiastical, had come to its full development, just previous to the Reformation. The human soul broke forth from profound darkness and captivity, with as sudden a glory as that which roused the shepherds on the plains of Bethlehem. And the hundred years preceding the Pilgrim period was one continuous outbreak and advance of the human mind towards Liberty! Scholarship was revived. Printing was bringing the democratic element to learning and intelligence. There was tumult in every department of society. The world had completed a full season, and was entering a new period. No one could then have so said. A darkness lay upon all men. In all the one hundred years in which the Reformation stands central not a prophet appeared!

The noble was borne he knew not whither; the king felt himself swinging at the anchor with an ever-lengthening cable; scholars found out truth as miners seek for ore, not knowing whether it should make sword or shield, buckler or knife, horse's shoe or nail for the sanctuary—as sawyers rip the deal log, thoughtless whether it is for the cradle or for the floor it rocks upon; for couch or for coffin. Men at that time were very earnest, intensely active, but every one with business right on hand. Divines were searching for truths, for immediate use against some cruel error, some pestilent persecuting dogma. The statesman was seizing a new truth, not from any foreseen relation of its system or philosophy, but because with something he must

# Puritanism

defend himself against intolerable pretensions of power. Scholars were not men of theory, weaving schools of modern days, who spin over the fields of learning with more webs than the sun shines upon in actual meadows. They were living men—men who felt yokes and burdens, and asked truth as knives to cut the stringent burden off. Kings disputed the very ground that men stood on, and sheer necessity drove them to find out a reason for their right to stand there. A common danger drove them to explore principles of right which should include all men in common. And so, the forms of development—civil and religious truth—naturally, and from circumstances of their origin, were towards the democratic or universal good. Everybody was made practical and wise by some existing necessity. All thinkers were held down to earth by the earthly movements. Men, like hounds, ran with their heads low to the ground which they coursed over! And as it was in Europe, so it was in England. As it was of the great army of Reformers, that secured to England her liberties, so it was with those who were broken off the parent tree to be grafted upon the wild stock of a wilderness.

Our fathers did not come hither on a speculation of philosophy, of religion, or of commerce. They came simply to be rid of oppression, and to live at peace with their own consciences. They never dreamed of future greatness.

The history of the Pilgrims is the proper epic of humility. They did not know their own worth, or suspect their own grandeur. They heard God's voice speaking in their age, and they obeyed it. It was a nice ear that could hear it. It was a pious soul that accepted it. It was a bold heart that could obey it. No Moses was with them. No miracle authenticated their moral convictions. No fire or cloud guided them. The invisible truth was their guide !

These men were of small account at home. If you will follow them back to their homes, you will now and then find a mansion, never a castle, but almost always a yeoman's house, or a labourer's hovel. At home the Puritans were weavers, cobblers, tinkers, merchants and mechanics. Only their leaders were educated. There is no evidence that they reared up in imagination any Promised Land, or that they fed their enthusiasm upon the visions of an ideal Republic. There was no Sir Thomas More among them, and they had no Utopia.

# Puritanism

There is no evidence of great foresight or foregoing sagacity in statesmanship. They were men of common sense in the affairs that lay near to them, but there is no evidence that they had the poetic glance or the in-looking eye of philosophy. But what was the state of an age in which the genteel men were able to be only courtiers, while cobblers and tinkers became statesmen, without knowing or pretending it? This is the lesson, then; that firm faith in God, and fidelity to moral truth in its application to the age in which men live, and to the business that lies next their hand, are the powers by which the greatest events are brought to pass.

In taking away from the Puritan the comprehensive glance that read the whole scope and future of the principles which he adopted, do we lower him in the scale of greatness? If he had seen the end from the beginning, he would have been more than a man. Not one of all those eminent names that acted in the Reformation were consistent with the since-discovered nature of the principles which they adopted. They accepted the doctrine of liberty with a local application. They never foresaw the logical future. Luther and his compeers vehemently denounced the Protestant war, although it was based upon the identical principles which led the Reformed Church to separate from Rome. That liberty of speech which the Protestant asserted as between Protestantism and Catholicism was denied by Luther, by Calvin, by Knox, as between different sects of the Protestant body.

The fatal notion of Unity which the Romish Church has for an iron centre was carried by the Protestant with the Reform. Despotism consolidates; Liberty opens, diffuses, relaxes. Growth in tyrannies is only petrifaction. Freedom develops as a tree does. First is the seed of some pine, dropped by the hand of frost, caught in the rift of some rock, and let down towards the scanty soil by the melting ice. It sprouts, and no voice announces its birth. It struggles for room. Its roots seek for nourishment from pervious rocks, and yet it thrives. And as it grows, it divides and divides again, united in the trunk but diverse in the boughs, until in full stature it lifts up ten thousand separate branches, each one with liberty, but all of them fibral, back to a common root.

But the knowledge of the safety which goes with diversity—the practical knowledge of it

# Puritanism

—belonged to a later period. And since it existed nowhere else, how should we demand it among the Puritans? Free speech with them was a self-defensory claim, and not a universal principle. Every man might revile the Pope—but the Quakers were forbid to revile the Protestant. That is as far as their experiment went. They believed in free speech, but beyond their own experience they dreaded it. It was reserved for their children to carry out to its full proportions this fundamental right of liberty.

It is the joy and glory of our age that this benign principle—liberty of the tongue—has dropped its blossoms upon our land, and that our hands are full of its fruits. For what are free ports, in and out of which ships of all nations may go, compared to the free mouth, which is the soul's port! And what is all the merchandise of gold and silver, of silks and spice, compared with the commerce of wisdom! Within, invisible, the all-skillful soul fashions her precious wares, weaves divine truths into governments for the nations, forges implements for sacred warfare, executes all conceits of beauty and of grace, and to the tongue she commits her treasures, as to a free and universal merchantman, that runs through

every latitude, and with endless rounds of
benefaction enriches the globe!

They planted the seed; we gather the fruit.
Now, the civilized world is yielding to a Puritan doctrine. Free speech is to the soul what
free air is to the body. To deny or suppress
it is to take sides with deceit and wickedness.
No righteous cause suffers by open search.
No cause dreads a Free Press unless it has
reason for dreading it. There is always a lie
or wrong when a probing tongue makes men
wince; and he that shuts a free man's mouth
would, if he had an opportunity, temptation
and impunity, shut the prison door upon him.
To shut up the tongue in his mouth is a worse
imprisonment than to shut his body in a
dungeon. But the Puritan was not omniscient.
He could not borrow the Divine power of
seeing the end from the beginning. Nor
should we blame him for knowing only those
stars which rose in his hemisphere.

Let us see, now, what was the Puritan's
Creed.

I. The first grand battle of the Puritan
was continental, and in behalf of the right of
every man to his own God. God is father,
man is child. Religion is liberty. No man
but the father shall tell the child what he may

do at home. The Church and the priests are helps, not masters. Ordinances are staffs, not sceptres. God gave to every man a telescope, through which he might see the eternal world and the invisible God. The cunning priest slipped in place of it a kaleidoscope, filled with bits of painted glass, beads and tinsel metals, and every turn gave fantastic figures and strange monkish devices, rarely fine to the superstitious, but disgusting to intelligent faith.

The first contest was simply this: Is the Bible a sufficient guide to God? Is the reason a sufficient guide through the Bible? Are an honest soul and virtuous heart sufficient guides for the reason?

Next, the magistrate sought to usurp the usurpation of the priest. King and Parliament undertook to direct the religious duties and worship of the subject. Against this in-trusion came the soul's Declaration of Independence, and, in England, this separation between Puritan and Churchman.

The last step taken into perfect liberty was that taken by the Independent, whose champion was Harry Vane, that one's own sect may not molest his free conscience.

That which the priest may not do the king must not. What the king must not do one's own neighbours and fellow citizens shall not. And here at length the Puritan emerged from the cave of darkness and into the hemisphere of light and liberty. It was the spectacle of the human soul claiming its birthright, asserting its sonship, inspired by full faith of its immortality.

II. But whatever gives strength to the soul for one purpose gives it universal growth. The rights of the soul against ecclesiastical domination could not fail to result in the same conflict with the civil magistracy. The logic that took the tiara from the pope's head removed the crown from the king. The Puritan shrank for a long time from consistency. They dared not follow their own principles. They strove to hold back. Like men who begin to explore some unknown river in a new land, that grew deeper and deeper at every league, until, like the Amazon, it seemed itself a sea, long before it reached the ocean, so were the Puritans upon that stream—the Liberty of the Individual! It was not until they had got out entirely from the shadow of the Cathedral that they could make straight lines in religion, and only when they left beyond the seas the whole fabric of monarchy that they gave consistency and symmetry to their civil governments. Before, the premises had been Government,—from which they strove to recover the rights of the people. In the wilderness of New England, the syllogism was reversed and the premise was the People—and the inference a government.

Only give the whole of a man to himself, and he is made to be prudent, virtuous, orderly, self-governing. This is the molecule, the atomic cell of Puritanism. Men need governments of restraint, just in proportion to the degree in which they are not developed and free. As the individual becomes educated and strong in his whole nature, moral and intellectual, he needs no government. For God made the human soul sufficient for all its own exigencies. It is a perfect state. It is competent to entire sovereignty.

The Puritan was a man thoroughly alive to liberty. Nor can he be understood or revered by any who do not believe as he did, that true manhood and Christian liberty were identical. The first effect of Christianity upon the world was monarchical and not democratic. It gave power to the intellect, and purity to the moral nature. But these were exerted in the direction of Government. In the sixteenth century there was in the world but one great interest

—Government. There was nothing else so divine, so worshipped. God was supposed to be revealed chiefly by Government. The world of ideas was pervaded with the idea of Government—Government—Government! Of the one hundred million people of Europe, God was supposed to think well only of about twenty thousand. The rest were used for the benefit of these.

Now in 1620, how stood the Puritan in comparison with the world? Just as the Primitive Christians had stood 1,600 years before. [At this point Mr. Beecher proceeded to consider at great length and with equal felicity, first, the relative conditions of Christianity and Idolatry, and second, the relative conditions of the Puritan and his notions of individual rights and monarchy with rights of Government. He then proceeded.]

The Puritan is pronounced vulgar. But by whom? Not by men who work. Not by men whose worth comes by character rather than station. He was the prophet of the common people, and was not ashamed to call them brethren. Why should the servant be more than the master? The Messiah was scorned as the son of a carpenter, who had never learned letters.

# Puritanism

The Puritan is charged with a frivolous zeal
against trifles—robes and linen vestments.
But were they trifles? Had they not meaning? It is in the power of association to print
more indelibly than types or the graver's tool.
Not what the loom made; it was not the linen,
but what the priest made it. It stood for
ideas. The homeliest peg that was ever driven
into the wall may hold up the warrior's armour,
or the king's robe. And days, trees, places,
garments, costumes may be nails on which the
heart hangs precious memories, or the imagination wondrous superstitions, or the faith earnest
beliefs. And the significance of any symbol
or ceremony is to be looked for, not in its intrinsic worth, but in the associations which it
carries to the popular mind. What is a wed-
ding-ring but a few pennyweights of gold?
Yet that little circle holds more to the wearer's
imagination than the horizon of the earth! A
king's crown is but a rim of gold. Yet who
can estimate the meaning of that word in the
world's history? It signifies law, authority,
obedience, the State, the world's sovereignty.
The gold band on the king's head may be an
iron shackle on the Commonwealth. A throne
is but a clumsy chair, but that chair is symbol
of all that men hold most august in authority

and worshipful in earthly reverence. And in the times of the Puritans a robe was more than a robe, and a linen surplice more than a garment. They carried with them the priest, the altar and the church to which they belonged. The Puritans cared little for the cloth, but much for the ideas which it symbolized.

They are charged with ascetic prejudices, and hatred of innocent amusements. But what are innocent amusements in a tyrant's hands? Shall a king defraud his people of political privileges and pay them in games and dances? If they would not question magistrate or priest they might have holidays, and masks, and bear baitings. What despot would not be glad to furnish amusements, if, for such an equivalent, the people would be content under all his oppressions? To-day, he of Gaeta would let his people dance if they would consent not to vote. He would pay for pipe and lute, if they would leave him throne and sceptre. But the sturdy sense of the Puritan despised the bribe, and cast it under foot. Revels and dances seemed to him but flowers upon the corpse of Liberty.

They are charged with indifference to beauty, and wanton desecration of art. But what was the art which they beheld? Not harmonious lines and wealth of colour. Art is language. It came to them speaking all the abominable doctrines of oppression. The more beautiful, the more dangerous. It was a siren. Its beauty was a lure. Did not the Puritans tread in the very steps of the primitive Christian? Was not Art, in the early day, but heathenism in its most potent and attractive form? The legend might be forgotten; the perilous mythology, let alone by one generation, would perish: but art stood aloft; gleaming in the tempest, radiant from thousands of pictures, silently fascinating and poisoning the soul through its most potent faculty—the imagination! And when the early Christian turned away from art, it was not because it was beautiful, but wicked. It embalmed corruption—it enshrined lies! And the Puritan lived in an age when the priest, the aristocrat, the king, had long and long been served by Art.

I doubt if in Cromwell's day there was a picture on the globe that had in it anything for the common people! The world's victories had all been king's victories—warrior's victories. Art was busy crowning monarchs, robing priests, or giving to the passions a garment of light in which to walk forth for mischief! Will any man point me to the picture of the wonderful number that Raphael painted or designed that had in it a sympathy for the common people? They are all hierarchic or monarchic. Michael Angelo was at heart a Republican. He loved the people's liberty and hated oppression. Yet, what single work records these sentiments? The gentle Correggio filled church, convent, and cathedral dome with wondrous riches of graceful forms; but common life found no signs of love, no help, no champion in him. The Venetian school, illustrious and marvellous, has left in art few signs of liberty, and yet where might we expect some recognition of the simple dignity of human life, if not in that Republic? No: her rich men had artists, her priests had artists, her common people had none.

In all the Italian schools probably not a picture had ever been painted that carried a welcome to the common people. To be sure, there were angels endless, and Madonnas and Holy Families without number; there were monkish legends turned into colour. Then there were heathen divinities enough to bring back the court of Olympia and put Jupiter again in place of Jehovah. But in this immense fertility—in this prodigious wealth of

# Puritanism

picture, statue, canvas and fresco—I know of nothing that served the common people. In art, as in literature—Government, Government, Government, was all, and People nothing. I know not that the Romanic world of art ever produced a democratic picture.

The Germanic World, from whence came all our personal and popular liberties, had a strong development of popular subjects in their schools of art. Their pictures teem with natural objects, with birds and cattle, with husbandry, with personals, and their life with domestic scenes and interiors.

What had an Englishman, if a commoner, to thank art for? Not a painter in England, from 1500 to 1700, until the days of Hogarth, ever expressed an idea which was not inspired by the aristocracy or the monarchy!

While, then, the Puritan stood forth under the inspiration of a new life in the state—the life of the common people—he had no thanks to render to art in the past. On the contrary, it stood against him. It plead for the oppressor. It deified the hierarchy. It clothed vice in radiant glory. It left homely industry, sterling integrity and democratic ethics without a line or hue. Every cathedral was to him a door to Rome. Every carved statue beckoned the superstitious soul to some pernicious error. Every altar-piece was a golden lie. Every window suborned the sun, and sent his rays to bear on a painted lie or a legendary superstition. With few exceptions, at that time of little influence, the art of all the world was the minion of monarchy, the servant of corrupted religion or the mistress of lust. It had brought nothing to the common people and much to their oppressors. When the Puritan broke the altar, it was not the carving that he hated, but the idea carved. It was not the window that he shattered, but the lie which it held in its gorgeous blazonries ; for nothing had any worth to the Puritan which was not morally sound, and which did not consent to Liberty.

It is all very well for us, who are without superstition, who cannot even understand the meaning of old art, to admire it and mourn over its destruction by iconoclastic Puritans. It is easy, after two centuries of experience, to send back good advice to those who struggled in the twilight of their beginning without help and desperately set upon by evils that threaten liberty, truth and love itself. Let us be glad that so little was destroyed, and wonder at the forbearance of outraged men that did so little injury to arts which carried deadly contagion to the popular imagination !

But why do I defend ?  Why do I interpret ? Their work is the best eulogy.  Do you ask for their sincerity ?  Go with these Pilgrims to exile !  Toss with them upon the deep !  Land with them on this December day upon the bleak New England shore—on this, the 22d of December, the shortest day of the calendar, but the longest day of American history, and most honoured.

They brought no gold; they found none. They found no dwellings.  No sunny clime cheered the weary voyagers ; no sweet fields sent forth a savour such as, even in winter, the south of England knows.  The hills were forested, but leafless, except the pine.  That stood green and hopeful, even in midwinter. That tree they marked.  They chose it for their banner.  It yet stands upon the seal of Massachusetts.  No symbol in heaven, or on earth, was half so fit.  What other tree so well can stand for the principle of Liberty ?  It grows without culture; it flourishes on soil that would starve another tree.  Sand or rocks are quite alike to it.  Every root is an engineer.  The mast rises straight up to God.  It spreads out its branches to the North, the

South, the East, the West, alike, and spires up in symmetry like a pinnacle of a cathedral. It defies the storm; is not afraid of heat or cold. It is grateful to culture, but thrives bravely even in neglect. It adorns the habitation of men, but is just as much the glory of the wilderness. And when all other trees have yielded to the frost, the evergreen pine lets go not a leaf, but holds up its plumed head like a warrior, and whoops and chants to the winds all winter long, just as it murmured and sang all summer. Is not that the tree of Liberty? The Pilgrims chose it—placed it on their banner. All hail to the Pilgrims' Pine—the tree of Liberty!

When they left, no one missed them. No king sat easier. No prime minister, Richelieu, or Mazarin, or Villiers, felt his care lighter. They were too mean. Gone or present, they were despised. Their doctrine was a pestilent heresy. The whole world scorned it. A few of the Puritans had become Pilgrims to a distant continent,—and that, wise men doubtless thought, would end the impertinence!

Two hundred and forty years! And what says the world now? England confesses that to the Puritan she owes her liberty. Their name is honoured. Men grow famous by merely praising them. Their principles, silently working, have ameliorated or changed laws and customs, until now England is one of the freest nations on the globe. Nowhere else is conscience more sacred from tyranny. The Press is free as the winds, and like them brings health by blowing. The tongue is loosed. Indeed, were the old Puritan suddenly to come to life again in Old England, so far has practice outrun even his utmost notions, that he would be in danger of conservatism.

And upon the Continent of Europe a complete revolution is effected. Those nations that have refused the Puritan principles are in their dotage. Spain, Portugal, Italy—where are they? Their life died down for want of using. They are the feeblest states in Europe. France, half Protestant, is becoming more free every year. The Emperor is no more monarch by the grace of God, but by the vote of the people![1] There are two centuries in that simple thing. And what is the schoolmaster of Europe teaching the indocile kings? That nations may drive out sovereigns who abuse the subjects' rights; that the people may choose their own rulers. Italy votes for her King! When votes are cast into the ballot-

[1] The reader will remember that this was 1860.

box before St. Peter's, the spirits of the old
Puritans will surely walk the streets of Rome,
and chant their airy psalms of praise. The
Czar signs the decree of emancipation in his
continental domains, and on the 1st of next
January, millions of serfs will enter the year,
freemen! Austria, sullen and reluctant, has
not the strength to defend her oppressed Prov-
inces. Asia and Africa are coming rapidly
under the dominion of nations which advance
the world in liberty.

And is our own land receding? Are we
unclothing ourselves of the garments of liberty, just as the nations are arising in its
robes? Are we about to put on the cast-off
rags of despotism, and join the oppressors
of the earth just when God is herding and
driving them from among men? No! Liberty was never loved more dearly than now.
There are more hearts that beat with intelligent enthusiasm for human rights than ever
before! And this night of Pilgrim celebration
had never before so wide and profound a sympathy! Our fathers lit a feeble natal fire upon
the rocks this night, two hundred and forty
years ago, and it has never gone out! It
burns there; it burns here; it burns in every
State in this Union; and will burn on for

ages yet. No vestal fire of ancient temples ever endured so long. No renewed candles ever glimmered so long before priestly shrines, as has glowed, and will glow, before the Puritan's flame—the freeman's fire!

The Germans have a legend that, on the anniversary of every great world-battle, the spirits of the old combatants rise and join again in silent glory above the scenes of their former conflict. To-night, methinks, the old Puritans of the 22d of December gather in high and solemn council over the scene of their landing. No war is in the soul—no sword is in their hand! A Divine glory is upon them, and with solemn benediction they stretch forth their shadowless hands towards all this Continent! And shall I seem extravagant if I believe that thither, through the high air, swoop the mighty dead of former days, to do them reverence—the Rutledges, the Pinckneys, the Jeffersons, the Madisons, the Franklins, the Adamses, the Hancocks, and all the revered names from every State that, with them, carried forward the Puritan work? Let us join them in sympathy. We send forth our hearts to-night to every American who loves the liberty which the Puritan planted on these shores! We greet, over all the earth, every man who stands boldly for the rights of men! We give our sympathy and our prayers to every man, wherever he may be, that is wronged and oppressed; and that prayer is and shall be, " God of our Fathers, send confusion to the oppressors, and liberty to the captive!"

## II

# THE WASTES AND BURDENS OF SOCIETY

SOCIETY is the most comprehensive of all institutions, the most complex. It is really the method under which men live together in all their interests, in their social relations, in their business, in their very various conditions of poverty, and riches, and industry. It is the largest subject that could be handled,—so large that when the subtler elements that enter into it are considered, no man can comprehend the whole of it. He can select departments, the moral elements, the political elements, the industrial elements, the intellectual elements; but there is in society something more than either or all of these put together.

In the human body there are hands, there are feet, there is a heart, and there is a head; but when the physiologist has enumerated every organ and all its functions, he has not yet described the man. Life is that subtle thing that no man can express and no man can understand; and so it is in that great organic body—Society. Under the providence of God it is an existence having within itself, though apparently much mixed and obscured, a life of its own. Its formation depends very much on climate, on the occupations of men, on the government and laws under which they live, upon the condition of religious beliefs that prevail among them, whether old or late in formation; yet, after all, with all these variations affected by incidental circumstances, there is something more than these enumerations indicate.

If you had never seen an acorn or any seed brought from a distant land, you might make a difference in its growth by the soil which you gave it, by the culture that followed it, by the climate in which it was brought forward; but after all there would be in that seed something that would not change; it would go right on from the germ to unfold itself as it pleased, according to the nature that was in the seed.

This is entirely set aside, apparently, by those men who are seeking to reconstruct society in the air upon the principle of some theory. They think that society as it has

been is very imperfect; so do I. They think
it may be made much better; so do I. They
think they have got the trick of doing it; and
I don't. They formulate this, and they formulate that, and after all society goes stumbling
on and has its own way. As if a naturalist
would think that an elephant was a great deal
too big, and that he was clumsy, and should
undertake to make elephants grow according
to his own idea of alertness and strength combined, as they are not in the elephant. Society is an unmanageable thing. Whatever
exertion you lay out on it will produce some
effect; yet it will not be the result of your
will, but the result that Nature gives to this
complex organization as it pleases her. Let
me then proceed, not to undertake to pro-
pound a new theory of what society ought to
be, but simply to do what every doctor does.
He can diagnose what is the health or sickness
of every individual, but he cannot reconstruct
it; he must act upon the lines of creation for
each individual. I can criticize, I can point
out wastes, I can show the burdens, and these
may successively be cut down by criticism,
and practically reduced in weight, in number,
in various ways; but this is very different
from undertaking to reconstruct society from

that foundation upon some notion of philosophy.

The first burden that I shall mention, the first waste, is *Sickness and Weakness*. Here and all the way through I beg you to understand that I am not discussing these topics, which in succession will come up, from the standpoint of humanity or morality, and still less from the standpoint of spiritual religion, but from the standpoint of political economy. That is the " science " which takes cognizance of the production of wealth, its distribution, and its uses in rendering society strong and happy, and I am speaking now in regard to each successive phase of waste and of burden from that point.

The proper duration of human life I suppose to be anywhere from eighty to a hundred years. Men are built so that they have a right to expect that. A man ought to be ashamed to die before he is seventy years old. But the average duration of human life is about thirty-three years. Consider what a waste that is, when society has in itself the power of prolonging life to a hundred years, or ninety years, or eighty years, and the average of the duration of life is but thirty, according to the old account, and thirty-three

now, according to the more modern estimate.
Well, here is two-thirds wasted; one-third
only does all the work that is done in human
society; and if you consider the period of
non-productiveness necessary in the development of childhood, and if you give to the aged
and outworn the liberty of some years on the
other side of life, and then count the productive forces, I think it may be said, taking
the world over, it is a fair estimate that one-
fourth of the human family do all the work
that is done, and support the other three-
fourths. Now, sickness is, from the standpoint of political economy, a squandering of
the forces of productive labour in human life.
No corporation, no commercial enterprise
could succeed,—they would go to smash, the
whole of them,—if they wasted three-fourths
of all their forces; but this great institu-
tion, Human Society, squanders three-fourths
of all its forces, yet steadily holds on
its way through time; in spite of all its
diseases and all its burdens and all its squan-
derings, it continues to exist; such are its vital
forces.

Now from the standpoint of political economy, weakness is worse than sickness, for if a
man has any self-respect when he is sick he

will either get well or he will die; but a man
that is weak will not do either. He not only
does nothing, but he hangs on the hands of
men who do take care of him, and, so far as
political economy is concerned, though add-
ing nothing he subtracts a good deal. From
the standpoint of affection it is a very different
question, but from the standpoint of the productiveness of mankind in political economy
it is a very fair question, so that weakness and
death are to be regarded as the wastes of the
industrial forces of human life.

One would not suppose, after the world has
had philosophy so long and has so much of it
now, that there would be any need, such as I
feel burdened with to-night, to set forth how
utterly inadequate men's ideas are in regard to
the maintenance and propagation of health.
There are two things that God made the most
of in this world that men are more afraid of
than of anything else—fresh air and cold
water. As regards this matter of fresh air : so
that a man can breathe, he seldom troubles
himself what it is he is breathing ; but nature
considers what it is that he is breathing all the
time. I have been speaking for more than
fifty years in every conceivable place—in
halls, in churches—and I have yet to meet

one single place where an audience ought to be detained for an hour.

A healthy man in the open air breathes about two thousand cubic feet of air an hour. Our best hospitals make arrangements for about twelve hundred feet per hour ; our best jails and penitentiaries make provision for about six hundred cubic feet per hour ; what the churches provide I do not know. The schools in the city of Philadelphia—and it is supposed to be a model city—provide for each child one hundred and fifty-six cubic feet per hour. In our schools in Brooklyn, where I live, fifty-nine, forty-five, thirty-nine, and, in one disgraceful instance, twenty-four cubic feet are provided for those little wretches that we call our children. If they had been thieves they would have got six hundred in jail. An audience gathered together in ordinary assembly-rooms not only have no considerable proportion of that air which they should have, but ordinarily in such an assembly-room as this, in about fifteen minutes the fresh air has been all used up once, and as there is very little resupply it will very soon be breathed over twice, three times, four times, five times, and in less than an hour every man, woman, and child in this assembly will have in him something of every other man, woman, and child. It is but very rarely that one sees a person who thinks so well of another that he would like to eat him up.

This vaporous intimacy with each other's interiors is not wholesome, and yet it is almost universal. The filth of it never seems to have struck anybody at all. If you were to invite a friend to your house, and put him into a bed where fifty men in succession had slept without any change of sheets, he would justly think you were a filthy householder, and you would have a right to be ashamed; or if you sat a man down to your table, and told him that ten men had eaten from that knife and fork and plate before he came in, he would not tolerate it for a moment: but yet in an audience-room they will go on eating each other over and over and over again without the slightest reluctance. Every man or woman in a congregation in half an hour has something in him of everybody else. But nobody thinks about it, and of all creation the men who think less about it than any others are architects. They make clean the outside and beautify the house, but within it is full of dead men's breaths, or the dead breaths of men.

Well, there has been an estimate formed in

# The Wastes and Burdens of Society

the United States, which I suppose will answer
substantially for Great Britain, as to the eco-
nomical value of a man. We estimate a man's
value in the United States as based upon the
fact that men earn upon an average six hundred
dollars a year, and a man's value is a capital
whose interest amounts to six hundred dollars
a year. Thus, every time an experienced
mechanic, every time a labouring farmer,
every time a productive citizen dies, the community loses the capital, whose annual interest
is six hundred dollars. Of course, when I am
called to a funeral I never look at it from that
standpoint. I never say, " Six hundred dollars
gone, brethren ! " Sentiment, taste, and religious feeling would prevent that ; but it is
gone, and gone very largely by the decease
of men whom society cannot afford to let go.
If an annual death of six hundred men in the
community had taken place, and they were
all shifty politicians, why, we could get along
all the better for their going. But one ingenious, inventive, skillful, and industrious
mechanic is worth a whole shoal of those in-
sects that fly about the community called
politicians.

Now it is the duty of every civic ruler to
look at this matter ; it is the duty of every

governing body, of Nation, State, county, town, city, to look after the health of the citizens, in draining, in lighting, in cleansing the streets, and in securing them from epidemics, or from the more gradual causes of sickness, and weakness, and death. And in doing this work it is indispensable, according to the dictates of the largest philosophy—and that is Christianity—that the care should be at the bottom of society, first and mainly, and not at the top. If you go into a community and see beautiful mansions, you have a right to rejoice in them. I like to see fine streets, well shaded; I like to see comfortable dwellings, surrounded by flowers, and all the elements of taste; but, after all, I can form no idea of the Christian civilization of any community till I go down and see where the working men live, where the mechanics live. The test of civilization is not at the top, it is the average, but more especially the bottom of society. They may be too weak to do it themselves, they may be too ignorant to do it themselves; it is, therefore, one of the highest duties of civic bodies to see to it that the great under-mass of human society are put and kept in conditions of health.

And there is also an appeal in this matter to

those that are able by reason of knowledge and of wealth to have ventilated dwellings and all the sanitary appliances of modern knowledge. It is right; but it is not the only thing that is right. No man can go home and shut his door and walk upon his royal carpets and say, "All things in my house conduce to health." Society is so knit together that the condition of the upper classes is very largely, though indirectly, determined by the condition of the under classes, and in no one respect more than in the matter of health; for, although they may seem to you brutal, there is no family so poor, there is no family so ignorant, there is no family so sottish that they cannot develop smallpox and malarial fevers. And when these ills are developed they do not stay at home; the wind carries them, they sweep through the whole community, and the neglect and indolence of the upper classes may return in the form of so-called Divine Providence through the development of epidemics by the under classes of society. For their own sake and for the sake of humanity every thinking man and citizen well off should see to it that the great body of society should be taken care of and that a preventable disease should not be allowed to ravage the community. It is pretty generally the custom in New England, where the winters are long, to have a great store of potatoes, cabbages, onions, and all manner of vegetables, and the old-fashioned way was, as soon as the climate became too severe for them to be left out in the open air, to put them in the cellars, which are built with thick walls, where they will not freeze. But when the spring begins to come on and the remnant of the vegetables begins to reek and germinate malarial influences, those silent, vaporous influences steal up through crack and cranny and partition. By and by one of the children is sick ; the doctor is sent for. He says : " It is singular that the child should have such a trouble as this ; if you lived in a squalid neighbourhood I could understand it, but this looks very much as if it were malarial disease." The child dies. By and by a second child is taken sick, and the wonder grows ; and the mother goes down, and by this time they send for the minister, and he looks grave. " Mysterious providence !" he says. Mysterious providence ! It is not providence at all : it is rotten onions and potatoes down-stairs. You cannot have a foul cellar and not have a dangerous up-stairs ; and in society the upper classes have a great deal more risk than they are apt to suppose; though they keep themselves in a sanative condition, yet there is this reeking influence that is coming up directly or indirectly from society everywhere.

The next burden and waste in society that I should mention is that which springs upon us from our *Parasites*. A parasite is an animal organized to get its living out of somebody else. It does not work; it sucks for a living. Of course, you know what a vegetable parasite is, like the mistletoe and certain air plants that live upon trees; and the insect parasite, the red spider, and the green aphis and aphides everywhere; we know what animal parasites are, intestinal or exterior; but the worst parasites in the world are human parasites, and society is full of them. All healthy men competent to work, but unwilling, who live upon society without giving an equivalent, I call parasites. The young man has had some ambition; he has run through his active energies, and he loiters about the streets morning and noon and night, and picks up a living, Providence may know how. All vicious men, and men that come to the legitimate results of vice, all criminal men that forsake industries and live by warfare, open or secret, I call parasites.

These that become the offscouring of communities, that ichorously drop from stage to stage, and at the bottom form a malarious mud —these parasites of society are wasters; and I have a right to denounce vice and crime and all the courses that lead to them, not alone upon high moral principle, not alone upon mere schedules of morality, but because they are my enemies and your enemies, and they bleed us and suck us; they are vermin that infest our bodies and our families. And if these classes are vicious, criminal, and parasitic, how much more are they that make them, those whose very trade and livelihood consist in making vicious and criminal parasites in a community! The men that make drunkards are worse than the drunkards. The men that make gamblers are worse than the gamblers. The men that furnish lust with its material are worse than those that are overcome by the lust.

And yet, when we preach a doctrine of restriction and ask for laws that should hold in these parasites of society, what a clamour is raised—we are interfering with the liberty of men; they have a right to support their families. Especially they say, " What has a minister got to do with this business? Why does not he attend to preaching the gospel of peace? Why does he come out and interfere so with the vocations of men in society?" I was a citizen before I was a minister, and I do it as a man and citizen, not as a professional minister; yet I would do it that way rather than let it go undone, for I am one of those who do not believe in that kind of minister that seems to be a cross between a man and a woman. There was a time when a man with a hectic cheek and sunken eye was supposed to be near heaven, and fitted to teach men and young men in the proportion in which he was going to the grave himself. Times are changed, and now robust and strong, open-eyed men are ministers because they are men, and have practical, humane thoughts and sympathies, living among men as men, and not lifted above men on some velvet shelf where by reason of their mere externals they are considered above and better than the average of human nature. Either way, I think it is the duty of every moral teacher to scourge the makers of crimes, and the men that invalidate the health or morality of the great body of the community. And there is another reason why I have a right to speak out. You declare that I have no right to meddle with other people's business; no, but I have a right to take care of my own business. My sons and daughters are dear to me, and when men do wrong about them by lures and temptations and snares, for humanity's sake as well as for parental affection and love I have a right to interfere.

And I hold that that is a sphere in which above all others a woman has a right to interfere. What are called woman's rights are simply the rights of human beings, and before a woman can do right and well in the direction of humanity and virtue she has a right to vote. In our land the vote is rapidly becoming the magister as things go with us, and more and more throughout all civilized countries the power of the vote is increasing. I hold that a woman has the right to vote; but if you withhold from her on any considerations of supposed propriety voting for the remote questions of civility, there is one sphere where a woman is not allowed to vote, and where she ought to vote. She brings forth children in pain, she spends her life on them, bringing them up from infancy and helplessness to manhood and strength; and if there is one creature on the earth that has a right to vote what sort of school there should be in a district, what teacher should be there, for how many months it should be kept open, what should be taught in it, if there is one person who has a right to speak of the gambling dens and drinking hells that are round about her family, it is the mother of the children, and in all police relations and educational matters and everything that touches the virtue and morality of society, our civilization will not be perfected until it should be, as it is in religion, that man and woman stand before God equal and alike.

There is another aspect of this matter of the criminal classes that is worthy a moment's consideration. It is industry that pays for laziness; it is virtue that pays for vice; it is law-abiding and God-fearing men that pay for unprincipled men's misdeeds. All the waste of society is endured by the virtuous elements in it. I am taxed, you are taxed heavily—taxed not for humanity in the care of the disabled poor—that tax we pay cheerfully; but you are taxed and I am taxed for the ignorance, for the vice, for the crime, for the laziness, of all the parasitic forces of human society. I am content when I am taxed by our law that applies equally to every one, but the pickpocket has no right to put his hand in my pocket; and the grog-seller has no right to levy taxes on me. The vices of society are the most arrogant of tax-gatherers; they lay the imposts themselves; they themselves declare how much men shall pay; they collect it themselves; you stand by and pay for the devil's wages.

The third waste that I shall mention is that which comes from *Ignorance*. It is a great loss to a man to have had a head put on him with nothing in it, and next to that it is a great misfortune to a man to have had a good deal put into his head and not know it is there. It is a curse to an ignorant man to be ignorant. If a man had no eyes, no ears, and no use of his tongue, he would be shut out from so much of knowledge, and every man would bemoan his condition and ask, " Why does he live?" But more than the eyes and the ears and the tongue are perpetually paralyzed in an ignorant man. Eyes he has, but he cannot see the length of his hand; ears he has, and all the finest sounds in creation escape him; a tongue he has, but it is cursed with blundering. An ignorant man is a man whom God packed up and men have not yet unfolded. If a man has as a mechanic a chest of tools and knows how to use a gimlet and a saw, and that is all, it is a great deprivation to him; he cannot keep up in the race of life; and an ignorant man must of necessity be dropping down, down to the bottom.

Society moves upon averages. To make society progressive, it is not enough to develop the top of it. In the dairy it may be all very well to have the cream on the top, but it is very poor in society to have the thing repeated; for society does not move by the force of its top: that influences some, but it is the average of the mass that either accelerates or retards the movements of society in advance. It is the hull and the freight, and not the sails alone, that determine the quickness of the voyage, and ignorance at the bottom of society benumbs society; it is obliged to drag this vast bulk. It is like a gouty man trying to walk; he may be good at the top and all the way down, but his feet are not good, and he cannot walk. It behooves, therefore, as a matter of political economy simply, that by schools and popular knowledge ignorance should be purged out from every community. There can be no prosperity deserving of that name that leaves at the bottom a section of ignorance nearly equal in numbers to that in the middle or top of society.

But chiefly it is the relation of ignorance to public affairs that I would emphasize,—the relation of ignorance in the production of property, and in that which concerns all property, legitimate legislation, and administration. In olden times, when there were but two classes in the state, one of which said: " Thus saith the king," and the other had nothing to do but to say: " Yea " and " Amen," the matter of political economy did not matter so very much. But with the growth of the ages the light that in early times shone only on the top of the mountain is finding its way down the mountainside lower and lower into the valley, and the inevitable course of the development of humanity is that the great under classes shall have some voice. At last we have come to a period in which it may be said of all the civilized nations of Europe and of America that the mass of the common people have gained such a twilight intelligence that they are partners in the administration of law and of government. Now where men holding the vote are really determinative of the best legislation, it is to the last degree important that they should have both knowledge and intelligence. I make a distinction between knowledge and intelligence. Intelligence is the capacity to see, to understand, to choose, to determine; it is an ever-active force; but knowledge is merely one of the fruits of intelligence—what it has found out. They are separable. I have known a great many men stop with knowledge, who could do nothing; I have known men that had intelligence and no education, and did a great deal. Best it is that both, large knowledge springing from active intelligence, should be the possession of every citizen.

Above all, we need that men should have the kind of education that should enable them to put themselves to their best uses. And this is an experiment that has been carried on in America. We hold here that it is a crime to allow a man or his children to grow up in ignorance—a crime against the Commonwealth. From the Atlantic Ocean to the Pacific, and from the Lakes on the North to the Gulf of Mexico on the South, there is not now a State nor a Territory, the population being either white or black, foreign immigrants or native-born citizens, in which there are not established free public schools. For it is held to be necessary for the existence of the Commonwealth that those who have the power of the vote shall have that power in the hands of intelligence, and for the conservation of the State itself. The State, the Commonwealth thereof, all of them determine that the people, as the first condition of citizenship, shall come up through the common schools of America, and no man pays one farthing for the instruction of his children in those schools, because the State cannot afford any other conditions for its rising population. More than that, we are making our common schools so good that comparatively few private paid schools can stand under them. And it is a good thing in another way, too ; it is a good thing for every class in society, however widely they may ultimately differ, to start together in a common citizenship. The children of the rich and the children of the poor sit together on the same bench. The rich man's dunce has no preference over the poor man's genius. Here is a clergyman's son, and right alongside of him the son of the clergyman's washerwoman, and oftentimes the last shall be first and the first last. Where there is to be a government of the people it is a good thing that for once in their life there shall be a level, and that the children shall stand on that democratic level all together and alike ; then let them shoot up just as far as their several talents will allow them.

# The Wastes and Burdens of Society

The next and fourth of the wastes that I shall mention is that of *Quarrelsomeness*, the bulldog nature of men. Darwin supposes that men descended, or ascended, rather, from the animal, and I think I have seen men that came through the wolf,—another man seems to have come through the bear, another through the fox, and some men through the hog, and I see some men that came through the bulldog. The excitement of life with them is some form of combating; they love to fight. Now the honest and temperate conflict, the attrition of mind with mind, the comparision of opinions and the proof of them in a gentle school of fencing, or the generous emulation of bodily athletics, is beneficial. The want of excitement is death. Excitement carried on from the basilar passions is bad; intellectual and moral excitements are the highest conditions of social life. But the kind of excitement that becomes quarrelsome and cruel has stood in the way of human progress for centuries, and it is not out of the way yet. For example, there are organized hindrances that stand upon quarrelsomeness and selfishness. In commerce competition, to a certain extent, is honest, but carried to excess it becomes quarrelsomeness. Men may, and often do, try to swallow up all those that are weaker than they. Up to a certain point competition is normal and wholesome, but beyond that point I think it is criminal. All attempts to restrict the liberty of men, and all violence in doing it, are criminal. I do not speak alone of governmental violence, but of legislative violence. I regard Free Trade as being the virtue of our age, and believe that oppressive taxations are quarrelling with the best interests of the whole of human society.

But all these things are not to be compared for one moment—the conflicts of politics, the fierce engendered strifes that grow out of it, the over-reaching, the under-reachings of men —all these secular things are not to be compared for one single moment as hindrances, with organized religious quarrelsomeness. About eighteen hundred years ago some inexpert angels came singing out of heaven, and their song or chant was : " On earth peace, good-will to men ! " But they looked down and saw what men were doing, and they flew back to heaven as quick as they could go, and never sang that song again. There never was so little of anything on earth as peace, and among those things that have destroyed it nothing has done more than organized religion. Religion as a creed or system has been one of the most ruthless or destructive of the influences that have ravaged human society. Turn back on the pages of history. Look at the wars that have sprung from creed differences ; look at the battles, the despotism, the racks, the inquisitions ; go through the bloody path in which the feet of the Prince of Peace, acting as Providential Governor of the world, has passed. Christ has trodden again Gethsemane, and that for two thousand years, and the chief advocates of His opposition have been those that were anointed and ordained to preach the principle of love and of peace. All the world, when the Greek Church and the great Catholic Church were at odds with each other, was inflamed. In both Churches—but more especially in the Catholic Church—what noble names ! what saintly women ! what admirable men ! what sweet literature ! And to-day, how it shows some of the noblest specimens of Christian life ! And yet, when you look upon its whole prolonged history, you see it smiting here and there by the sword, by fines, imprisonments, and in every other way. Religion was spoiled in its very fountain, and instead of its being love, the fulfilling of the law of the universe, it was simply infernal. In

those ages in which the Church organized itself to compel everybody to worship in some
one way, to believe in some one schedule of
doctrine, to declare themselves in affiliation
with any special line of organization, and some
of the protesting Reformers of the Church were
just as savage on those whom they called
heretics, I do not wonder that a man who was
a Christian after the New Testament idea was
noted as an infidel. Thousands of men have
turned away from religion organized, because
they were just and humane, because they loved
God and they loved their fellow men.

There are no more dungeons now in civilized lands where men are imprisoned for the
want of orthodoxy. No more are men burned,
no more are men exiled, no more are men
fined and their property confiscated. The
punishment has changed; but it has not been
destroyed. A more exquisite torture is where
you take a man's name away from him, and
his reputation, and make one sect stand over
against another with sneer and hissing, where
you make a man because he is of a different
Church from yourself a byword, and warn
men against him. The difference between
you and him may be on a point of abstract
philosophy, or it may turn on ornaments, or

on some mediæval doctrine; it is no excuse to say that a man that torments and punishes with moral intolerance believes it is necessary; it makes no difference what he believes. The man without the spirit of Christ may believe what he pleases, but he is anti-Christ.

The condition of sects is very rapidly improving. I have no objection to sects, denominations—have just as many as you mind to have, if you only teach them to behave themselves. A sect is under the same Christian law as an individual is. I have no right to go and see what time my neighbour has breakfast, though it differs from my time. I have no right to inspect his table and see what he eats and drinks; whole streets may live in amity and fellowship though they differ in a housekeeping way; they have perfect fellowship in secular things, but jealousies appear in all the elements that lie higher than that—in the realm of purity and love. The better day is advancing rapidly, for so large is becoming the sphere of mutual coöperative work in the reforms that are going on, that men who before would scarcely look at each other or walk on the same side of the street find themselves assembled on peace or temperance platforms, and, to their amazement, when they see a brother there, and look him over, he has neither horns nor hoofs. It is a great thing to bring men together. The effect of organized orthodoxy in days gone by has been to keep men apart. That was the theory of the Old Testament. To save men from idolatry and the infectious passions that belong to it, they were shut up in Palestine; but when Christ came, regarding the moral forces of religion as sufficiently strong to take care of themselves, He said to His disciples: " Go ye into all the world, and preach the Gospel to every creature." And the spirit of Christianity is one that spreads itself, accepts the universality of humanity, and tends to draw men to each other in creed and in church and in life. A procedure in this life that disintegrates and scatters moral and honest men is not Christian. By and by, when all the good that is in all the churches shall be confluent, and when men shall help each other by all that they agree in; when the things in which men agree—which are a hundred times more than those in which they disagree—shall come to the front and to the top, there is moral power enough in this world to make an advance of ages, as measured by the past.

# The Wastes and Burdens of Society

The fifth topic of waste and burden is the *Misfit of Men*. One thing is very certain, that no man can do his best work except along the line of his strongest faculties. Sometimes men ·do not know what is the line of their strongest faculties, and very often nobody else knows. And yet, when you look at society and the adaptations of men, this misfit of men to function is very pitiful. The best strength of men is often wasted. There are men most conscientious, most serenely sweet and pure and pious, digging and delving away in the pulpit where they are not fitted to be. A man that is fitted for the pulpit is a man who has the genius of moral ideas, and there are a great many men that have not the genius of moral ideas, or any other, and yet they are in the pulpit.

But did it ever occur to you that of all the mysteries in this world the greatest are not religious mysteries, not the Trinity, not Atonement, not Decrees, not Election, not any of these things? The mystery of this world is how men were created and shoved on to this globe, and let alone. Whatever has been revealed in Old or New Testament that tells of man, is that he has a brain, and that is a seat of intelligence, but it has been only within my memory that men have been taught that brains were of any use. Hundreds of men do not believe it yet. Ages went away before a man knew what the heart was for, or what it was doing. Men were not told in the early day, neither by writing on the heavens nor by words spoken by the prophet, nor was it made known by any philosophy, what was the structure of their own bodies, and the relation of their bodily condition to the outward world, which itself also was a wilderness of ideas. They had no idea of what was its organization; they were as perfectly helpless as a child in the nursery. It was through hundreds and thousands of years that men groped and groped and died, when medicine for their ills was right under their feet in the vegetable world; although there was the remedy no voice told them of it. What if I put a child on the foot-board of a locomotive and say: " Run this Flying Dutchman five hundred miles, and it will be death if you come to any accident." The human body is a more complicated piece of machinery than any engine; yet for ages and ages until our day men have had no considerable insight either into their own structure, or into the relations of the physical world, any more than into the highest problems that belong to morality or religion.

And, even now, when a young man of fifteen or sixteen wants to know what he is fit for, who can tell him? He goes to the doctor, who sounds his heart and lungs, and says: " You are healthy." " Well, what should a healthy young man do?" " Oh, you had better go to the schoolmaster." The schoolmaster says: " Are you advanced in mathematics? Do you know something about history and political economy?" " Yes; what would you recommend me to do for my livelihood?" " Well, anything that happens to come to hand." He can give him no direction. He goes to the minister, and his minister says to him: " Have you been baptized? Do you say your prayers every morning and night? Do you believe in the creed?" " Sir, what do you recommend me to do as my life business?" " Well, I commend you to Providence." The minister is as ignorant as the youth is—the blind leading the blind. In this condition of things, is it strange that men should take to their professions not from an elective affinity, not because they feel an impulse to run along the lines of their strongest faculties, but from ambition, or from the promise of gain, or from misguiding love? Here is a man, a bricklayer, and he has organized industry and acquired great wealth, and his family increases amain. His eldest son they set up in business, and he has inherited from his father business tact. The second son grows up, and the mother says: "Well now, James is a very conscientious boy, and I think we had better make a lawyer of him." They do, and he utterly fails. They say: "William?—William seems to have parts and has an interest in Nature: I think we had better make him a doctor. That is a very respectable calling—we will make a doctor of William. As to Thomas, he is not very strong in body, and he is not so bright in mind as the other children, but he is a good boy, he would make a good minister:" and so the parental idea is not, "What are my children fitted for?" but, "What is respectable? What will give them standing in the opinion of their fellow men?" Men are perpetually going to things that are above their capacity and other men in various conditions of life are toiling in spheres that are below their capacity.

What if a farmer should harness greyhounds together and plough with them? What if racing on the track was to be made by oxen?

# The Wastes and Burdens of Society

An ox is for strength, a greyhound for speed;
but men are greyhounds where they ought to
be oxen, and oxen where they ought to be
greyhounds, all their lives. How should they
know? By their blunders mostly. How
often most admirable men of ideas are mere
copyists! They generate thought, they have
latent poetry in them, they have latent
inspirations; if they had been put in the right
avenues, and under the right inspirations, these
men would have been great thinkers, and their
life like the outpouring of music. And there
are men on the judges' bench holding the court
who would have made good and excellent
farmers, and not a few men in the blacksmith
forge and in the stithy, or in the mines, who
would have been excellent citizens—influential
in all moral and civic affairs; but they are all
mixed up like a keg of nails. There is many
a labouring man that would have made a
good exhorter and a good preacher, and there
are many preachers that evidently were not
" called." When God calls a man to preach
He always calls an audience to go and hear
him. There is many a man thinks he has
heard a call, and doubtless he did, but it was
somebody else's call. I think I do not err
when I say that one-half of the energy of life

is badly applied, and that, too, which is adapted for the superior functions of human life. There has got to be a great light arise in that direction.

Then the next great mischief, which you will hear gratefully, because we always like to hear the faults discussed which we do not find in ourselves, is *Lying*. Craft is the remainder of the animal life that inheres in man, for weakness in the presence of strength is obliged to resort to craft, to dig under, to go sideways. Concealment belongs to weakness in the presence of despotic strength. Slavery always produces lying subjects, and in the struggle for life among men the weak seek to make up their deficiencies of strength by craft. And it is not always the weak either that do it, for men have an impression that truth, pure and unadulterated, is like twenty-two carat gold, too soft to wear ordinarily, and that it must be adulterated to about eighteen carat, and then it is tough enough to go. They say a judicious mixture between a truth and a lie is the true currency, and they do not believe in truth. On no subject in this world is there a greater lack of faith than in truth. You may have faith in the Transfiguration, and faith in immortality, but you have not faith in the safety of telling the truth everywhere and always.

I am one of those that believe the truth ought to be told whenever you tell anything. It is not necessary that a man should always tell everything, but whatever he tells, it is necessary that that should always be truth. A man has a right to concealment. The soul has no more business to go stark naked down the street than a man has to go stark naked as regards his body. It is the preservation of social life and of individual life, and the man that has not a great silence in him, a great reserve in him, is not half a man—he is a babbler, he leaks at the mouth. All this talk about benevolent lies, white lies, and the customary lies of society—I abhor the whole raff of it.

But men say, " Would you advise a physician to tell a man that he is going straight down to death ? " He will have to die, and lying will not prevent it. " But suppose a man were to come to your house for protection, and you conceal him there, and the soldiers are right after him in times of civil war, and they asked, ' Has So-and-so been here ? ' would you say, ' Yes, he was here ten hours ago ; we gave him a glass of milk ; he is in the forest, go after him and get him ; ' or would

you say, ' The man is hid in the house now ' ? "
Men say, " Would you betray him? Don't
you think it is right to lie for benevolence ? "
No, I do not. " Would you tell the truth to
a robber, when the life of your children de-
pended upon it ? " Probably not ; but that has
nothing to do with the principle. I may be
weak enough to tell a lie ; but that does not
justify a lie, nor me in telling it ; and when
you appeal to the weakness of a man to justify
a lie, you do not advance in any way towards
the truth. I hold that the hardest thing in
this world is for a man habitually to tell the
truth. A man who tells the truth is like a
man who lives in a glass house, and everybody
that goes by sees what he is doing there. A
man that tells the truth has to be very sym-
metrical in his character ; he has got to be
really a good man, and righteous, or he cannot
afford to tell the truth.

Now the political economy of the matter is
this, that lying disintegrates society. Men are
united together in the great interests of human
life by trust. On an average they believe
when a man says a thing ; when he says he
has done a thing they take it for granted. We
could not live if we could not believe in men.
" William, have you deposited those checks in

the bank?" "Yes, sir, I have." Maybe he has, maybe he has not; I will go round to the bank and see. " Has my clerk deposited checks for $1,000 in the bank to-day?" "Yes," says the teller, " he has." But there may be a collusion between him and some of the bank officers; I will go inside and see. " Is your teller to be believed when he says my clerk has deposited $1,000?" If a man had to do all that circumlocution in his business he would not have time to do anything else. We cannot get organized, combined strength unless a man is trusted, and the moment a man is known not to be trusted there begins the process of separation. The progress of all human life begins in the belief that men substantially tell the truth.

Men say society is full of lies. Yes, it is full of lies. There is a great deal of lying in all sorts of business; but the philosophy of that is at once exposed as false in this, that if lying were more common than speaking the truth, society would be like a heap of sand, it would fall apart. The cohesion is the belief in men's veracity. The fact is that a lie has to have a cutting edge of truth or it would not be worth anything. It is the truth that works a lie into anything like victory. On the street, in the shop, in the manufactory, on the ship, at home and abroad, the implication is that a man is to be relied upon for his word or bond, and if you take that away society goes back into original elements. Everything that tends to separate the confidence of man in man impedes business, and makes it more and more laborious. Truthfulness is general in society; but lying is too often used. The higher the proportion of truthfulness, the stronger the community. The permanent prosperity of society is to be derived not from the lower, basilar faculties but from the coronal qualities. All those influences, therefore, that tend to make the violation of a man's word and pledge easy ought to be swept out of society.

Then there is the false notion that men are more likely to tell the truth under oath than they are without an oath. A man that will not tell the truth without an oath won't tell the truth with an oath. You cannot make a man honest by machinery. There has got to be established in him an automatic honesty, an honest individuality. Therefore, I do not believe in the oaths of our courts. In the old days of superstition, men believed that by a reference to arms on the battle-field God would always decide for the right. That has been

exploded, and duels and conflicts for the sake
of truth are all gone into the lumber-room of
heathendom. And we may as well drop the
old superstition with regard to a man standing
before a mysterious Deity, and swearing on
the penalty of his soul, when he did not believe he had a soul, and did not believe there
was much penalty. And see how oaths have
passed into disrepute by the mode of prescrib-
ing them. Here is an honest, simple-hearted
man, who has never been in a court or through
a trial; he comes in rather tremulous, and
goes into the witness box. See how the clerk
administers the oath to him. He holds out
the Bible as if there was some emanation from
the Bible that would make the man tell truth.
But some witnesses would not swear and stick
to it on a Bible merely; the Bible must have
a cross on it; that gives it extra sanctity. Then
he is made to kiss it. Was there ever any
superstition more abject than that? Then the
clerk gets up and says to the man who is waiting to be honest: " In the case of John Doe
*vs.* Richard Roe you swear—mumble, mumble,
mumble, mumble." It gradually dawns on him
that he is sworn to tell the truth, the whole
truth, and nothing but the truth. Then the
lawyers on each side are determined he shall

not tell the truth, and that he shall lie, and when he goes off the stand he does not know whether he is on his head or his feet. That is called sifting the evidence.

I do not believe in Custom House oaths. I do not believe in Custom Houses anyhow. I think they are manufactories of lies. I have got to swear when I go back—I have felt like it many times, but I have got to do it—that I have nothing in my trunks or about me contrary to the customs laws of my country. I know nothing about the customs laws of my country ; I do not know whether they admit a jack-knife. I am wearing all new clothes, so I can say I have nothing but what I wear. It is inherent in the oath that it is morally weak. Every man who has to do with the Custom House has a clerk who swears for the firm, who goes down to the Custom House, and does the swearing there. These Custom House oaths are simply ridiculous.

But there is another kind of oath though not quite so frequent and perhaps not so demoralizing, yet hardly less disgraceful, when a green young man fresh from the college or the seminary, who has had his theology put into him as sausages are filled, goes before the council, or the conference, or the convention, or whatever may be the machine, and takes oath that he will preach the doctrines of the confession, or of the creed as they have been interpreted by his Church. For a year or two he does not know anything better than to go on doing it; but, by and by, what with books and collateral light, and intercourse with men, and the progress of science, the man begins to have wider thoughts, and very soon he sees that he cannot preach on that doctrine, so he holds his tongue about it. And there begins to rise from the horizon to him the bright and morning star—yea, it may be the very Sun of Righteousness; but he has taken an oath that he will not preach anything but what is in the book, as if a book ever contained the Lord God Almighty and all creation! What does he do? He compromises and holds his tongue, or else the conditions of fellowship are such that he sacrifices everything that is dear to a man. All his roots in the past and all social affections bind him to this particular communion; but for the sake of truth he suffers himself to be expatriated and cast out, and the world says: " If a man belongs to that denomination he ought to teach what the denomination believes or leave it;" as if there was nothing else than getting a salary, as if a man did not feel that the truth in his hands was the test of his allegiance to Almighty God. Ordination oaths lay men's consciences under bondage, for I hold, and the world will yet agree to it, that a godly life is orthodox, and no orthodoxy that does not carry love behind it is orthodox.

I pass on to the next waste, and I shall barely mention it and go forward, and that is *Drunkenness.* I specify this because civilization has developed the nerve-forces of mankind, and there is a physiological law now affirmed by scientific men, that a regulated stimulus prevents the waste of the nerve-matter which performs the function of life; that opium, hashish, brandy, alcoholic stimulants of every kind, and coffee and tea are, in moderation, nerve-conservators, and that the danger lies not so much in the article, as in the unconscious increase until the stimulants narcotize the nerve. That is the philosophy that, as civilization advances, men in the higher walks of life put forward. If a man can learn to love tobacco there is nothing on God's earth he cannot learn to love. Men are constantly seeking to reinforce nature in proportion as they are vigorous; but others say it is all wrong, that cold water and plain bread are

## The Wastes and Burdens of Society

better.  Every time you think or do anything,
a certain portion of the nerve is wasted in doing it; and if there be something that makes
the nerve tougher in use, that will explain the
almost universal use of stimulants.  What we
want to learn, if this be true, is to teach young
men and old men where the lines of safety be.
A man may be brought up in the rule of ab-
stinence, as I was; until I was sixty years of
age I never knew the taste of beer or of stimulants.  Since I was sixty-five I have known
something more—it is never too late to learn!
I am none the less a temperance man, for all
that.  I look upon the use of intoxicants
and stimulants by young men, or men in
health, as a waste, as well as a danger and a
temptation.

I would seek, not, however, by legislative
prohibition, but by moral persuasion, to bring
every man into a sound principle in regard to
self-control in what he eats and drinks, for I
do not believe there is any governing force
that is equal to self-government, and it is self-
government we should seek in every form of
life.  How is it that a young man goes out in
society?  He has been a tee-totaller at home,
but he goes out into fashionable society; they
set before him wines; little by little he begins

to drink. There is a great art in drinking, and a *bon vivant* knows what it is, and he can say, " Young man, if you are going to take any of this kind, let me tell you how and when;" but we do not dare put a young man to such instruction, so we let him go on and guzzle according to his own fancy. What we want to get is physiological knowledge and hygienic knowledge as to the proper use of stimulants. But men drink because they have an inherited appetite for drink; because they want to do two days' work in one; because they are of too slow and sluggish a temperament, and they want to wake up their slow forces and the inspiration of their mind; or they drink because they are in good fellowship. There are a variety of reasons. The result is, drunkenness spreads in all our communities. The moment a man has gone beyond the line of temperance he has lost his place as a producer in society and is a waste and a burden. Every church and every legislation and every form of public sentiment should limit the use of intoxicants and teach men to be temperate, for there is no evil that is committing so much crime; there is no evil that so populates the poorhouse, the jail, the gallows; there is no evil that takes away

# The Wastes and Burdens of Society

so much comfort from the home and makes so much misery therein; there is no one evil under the sun that is so infernal as that of drunkenness, for all other evils follow in its wake.

The last of the burdens of society that I would mention is *War*. This is simply animalism. I do not undertake to say that defensive wars, or other wars, are always morally wrong. As the world is constituted, physical force is often quite necessary. You cannot drive the team without some goad, or some whip, or some rein, or some harness. The animal must be controlled by animal forces, for there is nothing else influences it, and men are yet animals largely. When there are insurrections, and riots, and plunderings of property, and aggressions upon the peace and life of other men, there must be an arm stronger than their violence to hold them in. The theory that we are never to be allowed to use force would forbid police anywhere; and to forbid the hand of strength for the protection of the community is to give a premium to violence and lawlessness. But look at the history of the wars. The earth is red with blood. Look at the symbol of Great Britain— a lion; look at the symbol of America—an eagle; look at other symbols of nations—leopards. Men have rightly considered that the symbol that typifies the national life should be borrowed from animal violence.

I cannot say that the history of Great Britain would justify me in praising her for peace principles. I will admit that the tendency of British literature, and British religion and civility and polity, when men have been subdued, is benign, and develops a higher nationality everywhere, and that on her colonies and possessions around the earth, Britain has bestowed an equitable government and a procedure which is to the advantage of weak and dependent nations. But how came they weak and dependent?

In our own land I thank God we have been saved from foreign war, partly by our weakness, partly by the nature of our institutions, partly by our distance and exemption from the intercourse of nations; but in the pursuit of great principles we have gone through the baptism of blood, and we have come out with a national debt of hundreds of millions of dollars, and every dollar of it represents the industry of men. This counts nothing of the waste by the burning of dwellings, the burning of crops, the burning of fences, the up-

setting of society everywhere. The whole
South was made absolutely bankrupt by the
war in which she asserted a false principle.
I hold that there was never a people on earth
more sincere and honest in their conflict than
our Southern brethren ; I hold that they gave
their last dollar, their last breath, and when
they gave up there was nothing more with
which to make resistance. I bear witness
to them that as soon as they gave up they
gave up thoroughly, and came back into the
Union, and are now inspired with Union
principles as sincere as any in the North.
But this terrible internecine struggle was a
waste of a million of men. At Gettysburg
40,000 men lay dead, wounded, or dying on
both sides.

Can anything be considered more horrible
than the history of European wars ? The
wranglings of lions and tigers in the wilderness, the fights of the bear, or the cruelties of
the shark that kill not to consume, but for
savage destructiveness—human nature has been
more cruel than all the animal creation. The
days are coming, I think, when the best men
will not be called out for standing armies.
To-day Europe is armed to the teeth ; indeed,
the whole continent is a camp. All Germany

—it is not an army that they raise; it is an army that they are : and substantially that is the condition of France; and Italy, newly brought into the communion of saints of the nations, is still weighing down her population by the expenses for the army and navy. There is not a nation except Switzerland that dare lay down its arms. Yet they are all Christian nations. They would all be mortally offended if you said they were not members of the community of the Faith. Yet here comes in Christ's revelation of God's love, that rather than men should die He gave His only begotten Son to save them. Here comes that grand revelation of the eternities, that the test of love is how much men will suffer for others. Yet men are fighting for the love, slaughtering men for the peace of society, for the sake of obtaining the reign of the empire of love! Was there ever such a spectacle presented to mankind?

The general drift of many of you will be to say that I have given such a bad picture of the actual goings on of society that it discourages you. No. On the contrary, I think the world never was so much advanced as it is to-day. I think that it is the sensibility and consequence of this advance that makes the picture so vivid and so repulsive to you. Indeed, there is more of thought for the common people, for their external life, for their instruction, a larger conception of their rights, and more and more institutions that tend to fortify and extend the rights of the mass of mankind than ever before. I think there is coming on gradually a time when war itself will begin to be throttled. In that day may America be found leading, for the inducements and temptations to us are a thousandfold less than to any nation in Europe; and with us, and behind us—for there is no backing that we could covet like that of our mother country, speaking our language, from whose literature we learned, from whose religion we received inspiration, from whose legislation and sense of justice has sprung all that there is on the Western hemisphere—may Great Britain stand, and back America up in every step that she should take to make justice and equity comport with peace, and destroy war everywhere!

Professor Guyot says that there are three periods in the growth of a plant: the first is the longest and the most obscure—growth by the root; the second period is much accelerated— growth by the stem; and the third and fastest of all is the growth by the flower and the fruit. I take it, the civilized part of the world has been growing by the root through the centuries; and that we have come unto a time when the world is growing by the stem faster and faster; but that just before us in our children's day, and maybe in our own, society will burst out into blossom and begin to bear the fruits of righteousness as we have never seen it do in days that are gone.

Take no counsel, then, of crouching fear, still less of misanthropic cowardice. Take courage of this: there is a God, and He has time enough, and is not obliged, as man is, to run quickly through the offices of the building of His providence. He can wait through the ages, and He can wait through the junctures; but He is building, He is building, and that which His hand undertakes no man may long hinder. There shall be no man that shall have need to say to his brother, "Know the Lord!" for all men shall know Him, from the least unto the greatest. I shall behold Him, not here but there, in the midst of the rejoicing host; I shall understand that which to-day is an enigma, and I shall see the accomplishment of that in the midst of which I have striven, for which tears have been shed in ocean streams, for which blood has flowed through the race and through all time. The emancipation of man from his animal conditions shall be achieved before the race dies from off the face of the earth, and the glory of the Lord shall fill the earth as the waters fill the sea.

# III

## THE REIGN OF THE COMMON PEOPLE

IT has been the effect of modern investigation to throw light without illumination upon the most interesting period of human history. When the old chronology prevailed, and it was thought that this world was built about six thousand years ago, men had of necessity one way of looking at things ; but now it is agreed upon all hands that we cannot count the chronology of this world by thousands, more likely by millions of years.  Nor was the system of immediation in creation, which prevailed at the time, favourable to the discovery of truth. God who dwells in eternity has time enough to build worlds which require millions of years, and whatever may be the cause of the origin of the human race, and I have my opinion on that subject (confidential, however !), I think it may be said that the earliest appearance of man upon earth was in the savage condition.  He began as low down as he could and be a man rather than an animal.  This question of profound interest is one that can probably never be answered except by guess,—and guess is not philosophy altogether.

How did man emerge from that savage condition? There were then no schools, no churches, no prophets, no priests, no books, presses—nothing; wild tribes in the wild wilderness, how did they come towards civilization? You say that the first industries were those that supplied appetite—food, shelter, clothing. That is, doubtless, true, although we only infer it; but how did the brain which is the organ of the man begin to unfold, not the simple knowledge that lay close in the neighbourhood of every man, but how did it come to build institutions, found communities, and develop them, till now the human race in civilized countries are as far removed from their ancestors as their ancestors were from the animals below them? It is on this broad field that light falls, but not illumination. But later down, supposing that industries were educators, supposing that men were educated by war itself, by combinations requiring skill and leadership, by ten thousand forms of growing social life, by the love of property, the instinct that is fundamental to human nature—suppose that all this indirectly evolved the intelligence of the human family, how do we come at length to the period in which the unfolding of the hidden powers of the human soul became an object of direct instruction ?

The earliest attempt to develop men, on purpose, was in Egypt, so far as we know. The Egyptian school has in it all the marks of antiquity and of primitive development, for it was limited in the numbers admitted and in the topics taught. Only the royal family could go to the schools of Egypt. That included, of course, the priesthood ; and, putting aside some slight mathematical teaching, it is probable that mysteries and superstitions were the whole subjects taught—and that mainly to teach the higher class how to be hierarchs or rulers. When we cross over the sea to Greece, at a period much later, though how much we know not, we find that schools had developed, and that the idea of making more of men than natural law or the casual influences of human society make of them—the attempt directly to train intelligence and to produce knowledge was farther advanced, for anybody could go to a Greek school that had the means to pay—anybody but slaves and women ; they trained very near together in antiquity, and they are not quite far enough apart yet. But I am compelled to correct myself when I say that women were not privileged; they were. It is probable that in no period of human history has more pains been taken with the education of women than was taken in Greece; in all their accomplishments, in learning, in music, in the dance, in poetry, in literature, in history, in philosophy, even in statesmanship, women were very highly educated—provided they were to live the lives of courtesans. The fact is simply astounding that in the age of Pericles intelligence and accomplishments were associated with impudicity, and were the signs of it, and that ignorance and modesty were associated ideas. If a woman would have the credit of purity and uprightness in social relations she must be the drudge of the household, and if any woman appeared, radiant in personal beauty and accomplished, fitted for conversation with statesmen and philosophers, it was taken for granted that she was accessible.

We have a side-light thrown on this subject in the New Testament, not well understood hitherto. That noble old Jewish book, the Bible, reveals a higher station to womanhood in the ancient Israelitish days than in any

other Oriental land, and from the beginning
of the Old Testament to the end of it there is
no limitation of a woman's rights, her functions and her position. She actually was
public in the sense of honour and function;
she went with unveiled face if she pleased;
she partook of religious services and led
them; she was a judge, she was even a leader
of armies; and you shall not find, either in
the Old Testament or in the New, one word
that limits the position of a woman till you
come to the Apostle's writings about Grecian
women, for only in *Corinthians* and in the
writings of Paul to Timothy, who was the
Bishop of the Greek Churches in Asia Minor,
do you find any limitation made. Knowing
full well what this public sentiment was at that
time, Paul said: " Suffer not a woman to teach
in your assemblies; let your women keep
silence." Why? because all, in that corrupt
public sentiment, looking upon intelligent
teachers in the Christian Church, would have
gone away and said: " This is done of licen-
tiousness, women are teaching;" and in a
public sentiment that associated intelligence
and immorality it is not strange that pruden-
tially and temporarily, women were restrained.

But that has all gone; woman has risen;

not only in intelligence, she is the universal teacher, not alone in the household but in the school; not alone in common schools but in every grade; till she has attained professorships in universities and even presidency in women's colleges—at least in our land. She is the right hand of the charities of the Church; she walks unblushing with an unveiled face where men do walk; and she is not only permitted in the great orthodox churches of New England to speak in meeting, but when they send her abroad, ordained to teach the Gospel to the heathen, there she is permitted to preach. When they come home women may still teach in a hall, but not often in a church, for dear old men there are yet so conservative that they are reading through golden spectacles their Bibles, and saying: " I suffer not a woman to preach."

We hardly can trace the unfolding of human intelligence after it plunged into that twilight or darkness of the Middle Ages. Then we begin to find intelligence developed through mechanical guilds, and in various ways of commerce; schools, such as we now understand schools to be, are very imperfectly traced out in the Middle Ages. But when that new impulse came to the moral nature, and the civil nature, and the intellectual and philosophical nature, to art, literature, to learning—when the Reformation came, whose scope was not ecclesiastical alone by any means—it was a resurrection of the human intelligence throughout its whole vast domain—schools began to appear to be, as John Milton says,

Raked embers out of the ashes of the past,

and they began to glow again. And from that time on, when men made efforts to develop by actual teaching, human intelligence grows broader, brighter and more effectual down to our present time ; and to-day in the principal nations of Europe education is compulsory, the education not of favoured classes, not of the children of the wealthy, not of those that have inherited genius, but the children of the common people. It is held that it is unsafe for a state to raise ignorant men. Ignorant men are like bombs, which are a great deal better to be shot into an enemy's camp than to be kept at home, for where an ignorant man goes off he scatters desolation. Moreover, an ignorant man is an animal, and the stronger his passions and the feebler his conscience and intellect, the more dangerous he is. Therefore, for the sake of the commonwealth, modern legislators wisely, whether they guide republican institutions or monarchical institutions or aristocratical institutions, have at last joined hands on one thing—that it is best to educate the people's children, from the highest to the lowest everywhere.

And what, in connection with various other general causes, has been the result of this unfolding of intelligence among the common people? It has not yet gone down to the bottom; there is a stratum of undeveloped intelligence among the nations, certainly; I am not speaking now of the residuum that falls down from the top like the slime of the ocean, but of those who are reasonable and honest and virtuous and useful. It may be said that, as the sun touches the tops of the mountains first and works its way downward through the valley later and later in the day, so there is very much to be done yet to bear knowledge and intelligence, which is better than knowledge, to the lowest classes of the common people. But even in this condition, what has been the result in Europe of the education of the common people? All those heavings, all those threatened revolutions, all those civil and commercial developments that are like the waves of the sea, are springing from the fact that God

in His providence has thrown light and intelligence upon the great undermass of society;
and the underparts of society, less fortunate in
every respect than those that are advanced,
are seeking room to develop themselves; they
are seeking to go up, and no road has been
found along which they can travel far as yet.
I do not believe in Nihilism in Russia, but if I
had been born and brought up there and had
felt the heel on my neck, I would have been a
Nihilist. I am poor stuff to make an obedient
slave out of. Nevertheless, they are like blind
men trying to find their way into the open air,
and if they stumble or go into wrong departments, are they to be derided and cursed?
Because they are seeking to construct a government after they shall have destroyed government and made a wilderness, are they,
while they are doing the best they know how
—are they, therefore, to be cursed, or rather
to be pitied, better directed, emancipated?
When they come to America to teach us how
to make commonwealths we think they are out
of place, decidedly. We thank Europe for a
great deal—for literature, ancient and modern;
we thank Europe for teachers in art, in colour,
in form, in sound, we are grateful for all these
things; but when the Socialists of Germany,

and the Communists of France, and the Nihilists of Russia come to teach us how to reorganize human society, they have come to the wrong place. Their ignorance is not our enlightenment.

The main cause of all the disturbance during the last half-century—the cause of causes—lies in the swelling of the intelligence of the great, hitherto neglected, and ignorant masses of Europe; they are seeking elevation, they are seeking a larger life, and as men grow in intelligence life must grow too. When a man is mere animal he does not want much except straw and fodder; but when a man begins to be a rational and intelligent creature, he wants a good deal more than the belly asks; for reason wants something, taste needs something, conscience craves something, every faculty brought into ascendancy and power is a new hunger, and must be supplied. No man is so cheap as the brutal, ignorant man; no man can rise up from the lower stations of life and not need more for his support from the fact that he is civilized and Christianized, and although he may not have it individually, the community must supply it for him. He must have resources of knowledge, he must have means of refinement, he must have limitations of taste or he feels himself slipping back. As I look upon the phenomena of society in Europe I see them as the phenomena of God. He is calling to the great masses of a growingly enlightened people, " Come up," and they are saying, " Which way ? By what road ? How ? " They must needs pass through the experiment of ignorance, tentative ignorance, and failure in a thousand things—they must pass through these preliminary stages, for as it was necessary when they came out of the bondage of Egypt that the children of Israel should go through the wilderness for forty years, so all people have to go forty years and more through the wilderness of mistake, the wilderness of blind trails and attempts that fail. It may be said, indeed, that the pyramid of permanent society is built up on blocks of blunders ; mistakes have pointed out the true way to mankind.

Now what has taken place among the common people ? Once they thought only about their own cottage, and their own little steading ; they have gradually learned to think about the whole neighbourhood. Once they were able to look only after their own limited affairs ; they begin to recognize the community of men, and to think about the affairs of others,

—as the Apostle said : " Look ye every man on his own things, but also every man on the things of others." They are having a society interest among themselves. Once they had limited thoughts and bits of knowledge ; now they have the mother of knowledge—intelligence : they are competent to think, to choose discriminately ; they are competent to organize themselves ; they are learning that self-denial by which men can work in masses ; they are beginning to have a light in life transcendently higher than the old contentment of the bestial state of miserable labour.

Such are the results, briefly stated, to which God in His providence has brought the masses of the European common people, and the promise of the future is brighter even than the fulfillment of the past. What the issues will be, and what the final fruits, God knows and man does not know !

Now if we examine these matters as they are in America, we shall find that there are influences tending to give more power to the brain, alertness, quickness, to give to it also a wider scope and range, than it has in the average of the labouring classes in Europe. Our climate is stimulating. Shipmasters tell me that they cannot drink in New York as they do in Liverpool. (Heaven help Liverpool!) There is more oxygen in our air. It has some importance in this, that anything that gives acuteness, vivacity, spring, to the substance of the brain prepares it for education and larger intelligence. A dull, watery, sluggish brain may do for a Conservative; but God never made them to be the fathers of progress. They are very useful as brakes on the wheel down-hill; but they never would draw anything up-hill in the world. And yet, in the climatic influence that tends to give vitality and quickness, force, and continuity to the human brain, lies the hope for a higher style of manhood; although it is not to be considered as a primary and chief cause of " smartness," if you will allow that word, yet it is one among others. And then, when the child is born in America, he is born into an atmosphere of expectation. He is not out of the cradle before he learns that he has got to earn his own living; he is hereditarily inspired with the idea of getting on in the world. Sometimes, when I see babies in the cradle apparently pawing the air, I think that they are making change in their own minds of future bargains. But this has great force as an educating element in early childhood:

# The Reign of the Common People

" You will be poor if you do not exert yourself : " and at every future stage circumstances
make it clear that it lies with each man what
his condition in society is to be.    This becomes
a very powerful developer of the cerebral
mass, and from it come intelligence and the
power of intellect.   And then, beyond that,
when the man goes into life the whole style of
society tends towards intense cerebral excita-
bility.   For instance, as to business, I found in
London that you may go down at nine o'clock
to see a man and there is nobody in his office ;
at ten o'clock the clerks are there ; at eleven
o'clock some persons do begin to appear.   By
that time the Yankees have got half through
the day.

This is in excess with us : it is carried to a
fault; for our men are ridden by two demons.
First, they desire excessive property—I do not
know that they are much distinguished from
their ancestors—they desire more than enough
for the uses of the family ; and when a man
wants more money than he can use, he wants
too much.   But they have the ambition of
property, which is accursed, or should be.
Property may be used in large masses to develop property, and coördinated estates may
do work that single estates cannot do; I am

not, therefore, speaking of vast enterprises like railroads and factories. But the individual man thinks in the beginning, " If I could only make myself worth a hundred thousand dollars, I should be willing to retire from business." Not a bit of it! A hundred thousand dollars is only an index of five hundred thousand; and when he has come to five hundred thousand he is like Moses—and very unlike him—standing on the top of the mountain and looking over the promised land, and he says to himself, " A million! a million!" And a million draws another million, until at last he has more than he can use, more than is useful for him, and many a one won't give it away— not till after his death. That is cheap benevolence. Well, this is the first element of mistake among large classes of commercial life in America.

The second is, they want it suddenly. They are not willing to say, " For forty years I will lay gradually the foundations, and build the golden stores one above another." No; they want to win quickly, by gambling, for that is gambling when a man wants money without having given a fair equivalent for it. And so they press nature to her utmost limits till the very diseases of our land are changing; men are dropping dead—it is heart disease; men are dropping dead—it is paralysis; men are dropping dead—it is Bright's disease. Ah! it is the violence done to the brain by excessive industry, through excessive hours, and through excessive ambition, which is but another name for excessive avarice.

But outside of that there is still another excitement, and that is politics. Now, the English in their insular and cool climate are rarely excited in politics, but we are in our sunshiny land; especially are we so once in four years, when the great quadrennial Presidential election comes off, and when the most useless thing on God's earth is built on God's earth—namely, a political platform, which men never use and never stand on after it is once built. Then the candidates are put forth, and every newspaper editor, and every public-spirited citizen and elector, goes before the people and declares to them that the further existence of the Government depends on the election of both parties. Now nations have a wondrous way of continuing to live after they are doomed to death, and we contrive to get along from four years to four years; nevertheless the excitement is prodigious. Men say these wild excitements are not wholesome, I say they are the best things that can happen to the community. I say the best speeches of the community scattered through the land, discussing finance, taxes, education, are the education of the common people, and they learn more in a year of universal debate than they would in twenty years of reading and thinking without such help.

Well, outside of that there is still another excitement, and that is in the Church, which is the hottest place of all. I do not mean a torrid heat; I do not mean a fuliginous kind of heat; I mean simply this that, even under its poorest administration, religion brings to bear upon the human brain the most permanent and the most profound excitements that are known to humanity. If you take denominations as they are now, you could not illustrate much by them, for they are mere incidents in the history of time, and they are no permanent, cohesive, systematic developments. I divide all Christian denominations into three sections: those that work by doctrines; those that work by emotion; and those that work by devotion. The men that work by doctrines think they have found out the universe; they have not only got it, but they have formulated it: they know all about the Infinite, they have sailed round Eternity, they know all about the Eternal and the Everlasting God, and you will hear them discuss questions of theology: " Now God could not, consistent with consistency, do so-and-so." They know all His difficulties ; they know how He got round them. One might easily come to think that God was their next-door neighbour. Well, after all, whether it is true or false, their systematic views, their dogmas, are really important to teach young and middle-aged and old to attempt, by philosophic reasoning, to reach into these unfathomable depths. It produces a power upon the brain of most transcendent importance. The dogmatists in their way may not increase the sum of human knowledge, but they increase the capacity of the human brain for profound thought and investigation, and that is wholesome and helpful.

Then there are the joyous churches, that love hallelujahs, songs, hymns—revival churches, Moody and Sankey movements, Methodist movements of all kinds, the Salvation Army, which has done noble work among the people. I need not undertake to show you that this emotion also tends to produce cerebral activity, and has an educating force in regard to the facility with which the brain acts.

Then there come those churches that live in an atmosphere of devotion, formulated prayers printed services. One would not think that stereotyped prayers read in the dim light of a painted window would produce great conflagration! Nor, indeed, do they. But when you come to look at the interior life of these churches, you shall find that their charities, their sense of responsibility to the weak and the poor and the ignorant, are perpetually acting as an inward fire, and developing intelligence in ways not common to the other forms of religious worship.

Well, what has been the result of all these influences which have been superadded to those universal stimuli to which all the civilized world outside of our land has been subject? We have 60,000,000 men, women, and children in America; we have common schools for every living soul that is born on this continent—except the Chinese. Now, in the States where twenty-five years ago it was a penitentiary offense to teach a slave how to read, we are sending out educated coloured men and women to teach, to preach, to practice law and medicine through the coloured population of the South; the Government is enlisted in their behalf, and the States are proud

of their coloured schools, that a little time ago
would have burnt a man who dared to advocate the education of the slave. We are the
harbour to which all the sails of the world
crowd with emigrants, and we bless God for it.
Their letters go back thicker than leaves in
autumn, to those that are left behind; and we
have a vast population from Spain, from Portugal, from Italy, from Hungary, from Austria,
from Germany, from Russia; we have a vast
population from all the Scandinavian lands,
from Scotland, from England, and occasionally
from Ireland. Let them come! It takes a
little time to get them used to things; but
whenever the children of foreign emigrants, of
whom we have 8,000,000 born and bred in
our land—whenever those children have gone
through our common schools, they are just as
good Americans as if they had not had foreign
parents. The common schools are the stom-
achs of the Republic, and when a man goes in
there he comes out, after all, American.

Well, now, we are trying this experiment
before the world on a tremendous scale, and
the world does not quite believe in it. I do.
They say: " With regard to your success in
government of the people by the people for
the people, you are dependent upon extraneous

conditions; it is not philosophically to be
inferred from the principles of your government; you have got so much land that it's
easy now; wait till the struggle for existence
takes place, as in the denser populations of
Europe, and then you will find that self-government will be but flimsy to hold men's
passions in check. By and by, you will go
from anarchy to a strong centralized Government." I do not blame them for thinking so.
If I had been brought up as they have been,
perhaps I should think so; but they do not
understand the facts which actually are in
existence, and are fundamental. For we are
not attempting to build Society; we are by
Society attempting to build the individual.
We hold that the State is strong in the proportion in which every individual in that State
is free, large, independent. Europe has a
finer educated upper class than we have;
noble and deep scholars in greater numbers
than we; institutions compared with which
ours are puny. Europe is educating the top;
we are educating society from the bottom to
the top. We are not attempting to lift favoured classes higher; we are not attempting
to give to those that already have; we are
attempting to put our hands under the foun-

dations of human life, and lift everybody up. That is a slower work; but when it is done, the world will never doubt again which is the wisest and best policy.

I do not suppose that one looking from the outside upon the experiment of self-government in America would have a very high opinion of it. I have not either, if I just look on the surface of things. Why, men will say: " It stands to reason that 60,000,000 ignorant of law, ignorant of constitutional history, ignorant of jurisprudence, of finance, and taxes and tariffs and forms of currency; 60,000,000 people that never studied these things—are not fit to rule. Your diplomacy is as complicated as ours, and it is the most complicated on earth, for all things grow in complexity as they develop towards a higher condition. What fitness is there in these people?" Well, it is not democracy merely; it is a representative democracy. Our people do not vote in mass for anything; they pick out captains of thought, they pick out the men that do know, and they send them to the Legislature to think for them, and then the people afterwards ratify or disallow them.

But when you come to the Legislatures I am bound to confess that the thing does not look very much more cheering on the outside. *Do the people really select the best men?* Yes: in times of danger they do very generally, but in ordinary time " kissing goes by favour." *What is that dandy in the Legislature for?* Oh, his father was an eminent judge, and they thought it would be a compliment to the old gentleman to send his son up to the Legislature,—not because he knows anything, but because his father does. It won't do to make too close an inquisition as to why people are in Legislatures. *What is that weazel-faced lawyer doing there?* Well, there may be ten or twenty gentlemen who wanted legislation that would favour their particular property interest instead of the Commonwealth, and they wanted somebody to wriggle a bill through the Legislature, and so he sits for the Commonwealth. *That great blustrous man squeezing on the front seat; what is he there for?* He? He could shake hands with more mothers, kiss more pretty girls and more babies, and tell more funny stories in an hour than any other man in a month, and so they send him up to make laws. When they get there it would do your heart good just to go and look at them. You know what the first duty of a regular Republican-Democratic legislator is. It is to get back again next winter. His second duty is what? His second duty is to put himself under that extraordinary providence that takes care of legislators' salaries. The old miracle of the prophet and the meal and the oil is outdone immeasurably in our days, for they go there poor one year, and go home rich; in four years they become money-lenders, all by a trust in that gracious providence that takes care of legislators' salaries. Their next duty after that is to serve the party that sent them up; and then, if there is anything left of them, it belongs to the Commonwealth. Some one has said, very wisely, that if a man travelling wishes to relish his dinner he had better not go into the kitchen to see where it is being cooked; if any man wishes to respect and obey the law, he had better not go to the Legislature to see where it is prepared. (This, I presume, is entirely an American point of view—without parallel in other lands!)

There are a great many more faults in self-government, but time will not permit me to enumerate them all; and yet I say that self-government is the best government that ever existed on the face of the earth. How should that be, with all these damaging facts? " By their fruits ye shall know them." What a government is is to be determined by the kind of people it raises, and I will defy the whole world in time past, and in time present, to show so vast a proportion of citizens so well off, so contented, so remunerated by their toil. The average of happiness under our self-government is greater than it ever has been, or can be, found under any sky, or in any period of human history. And the philosophical reason is not far to find; it belongs to that category in which a worse thing is sometimes a great deal better than a better thing.

William has been to school for more than a year, and his teacher says to him one day: " Now, William, I am afraid your father will think that I am not doing well by you; you must write a composition—you must send your father a good composition to show what you are doing." Well, William never did write a composition, and he does not know how. " O, write about something that you do know about—write about your father's farm," and so being goaded to his task, William says: " A cow is a useful animal. A cow has four legs and two horns. A cow gives good milk. I love good milk. William Bradshaw."

# The Reign of the Common People

The master looks over his shoulder, and says:
" Pooh! your father will think *you* are a cow.
Here, give me that composition, I'll fix it."
So he takes it home and fixes it. Here it
reads: " When the sun casts off the dusky
garments of the night, and appearing o'er the
orient hills, sips the dewdrops pendant from
every leaf, the milkmaid goes afield chanting
her matin song," and so on, and so on. Now
while, rhetorically, the master's composition
was unspeakably better than William's, as a
part of William's education, his own poor
scrawly lines are unspeakably better than the
one that has been " fixed " for him. No man
ever yet learned by having somebody else learn
for him. A man learns arithmetic by blunder
in and blunder out, but at last he gets it. A
man learns to write through scrawling; a man
learns to swim by going into the water; and
a man learns to vote by voting. Now we are
not attempting to make a Government; we
are attempting to teach sixty millions of men
how to conduct a Government by self-control,
by knowledge, by intelligence, by fair opportunity to practice. It is better that we should
have sixty millions of men learning through
their own mistakes how to govern themselves,
than it is to have an arbitrary Government

with the whole of the rest of the people ignorant.

Thus far I have spoken of the development
of the common people in their relations to
political economy and to government and
politics, but I have left out the more important, the less traversed part. I affirm that the
intelligence of the great mass of the common
people has a direct bearing upon science, upon
art, upon morality, upon religion itself. It
would not seem as though the men that were
superior in education and knowledge could receive anything from those below. Perhaps
No; perhaps Yes; for that which education
gives is more nearly artificial than that which
is inspired by the dominant sense and condition of the human mind that unites people in
greater mass. Why, two hundred years ago,
there was but one doctor in the village; nobody but him knew anything of medicine.
To-day hygiene, physiology, are taught in our
schools, are spread abroad by newspapers or
in lectures, or from the pulpit, and the common
people in our land have their dividends of
human knowledge. A woman that has brought
up six children knows more about medicine
than the village doctor did two hundred years
ago. Two centuries ago, nobody knew any-

thing about law but the judge and the councillors. To-day everybody knows something about law. We have broken open the arcana, we have distributed its treasures of knowledge, and the labourer knows something about law, the farmer, the mechanic, the merchant— everybody has an elementary knowledge of law. Has it destroyed the profession of the law? There never were so many highly educated men as now in the profession of the law, never were they more trustworthy and honourable, never had larger interests put into their hands, never had larger fees, and never were more willing to have them than they are now. They do not suffer by the intelligence of the common people which comes from distribution of the elementary forms of professional knowledge.

How, then, is it with regard to the Church? Just the same ; just the same. Three hundred years ago there was but one Bible in a parish in England, and that was chained to a column in the church ; and there was but one man to read it—the priest. And the people did not understand it then, and it was a part of official duty to go from house to house on the theory that the average parent did not know enough to teach the children the first principles of morality and religion. Go to-day over the same community or a like community in America, and on the Sabbath morning you shall see the girls and the young men with Bibles under their arms, themselves teachers, going to mission schools, going down to instruct their mental inferiors. The clergy has distributed its functions among the common people. Has that destroyed the profession? It never was stronger, never was as strong as it is to-day. Thank God, as to mere professional power, save by ordination, save by some endowment from without, there never was a time since the Advent when the clergy had so little influence as they have to-day: and it is growing less and less, and with the ages they will grow so pale that they cannot cast a shadow. Yet there never was a time when the man of God—because he was moved by the Holy Spirit of God to unfold his own moral consciousness, living among men, tied to them by no other ties than the sympathies of love—there never was a time when he had so much influence as to-day. And let me say that with regard to the ministers of the Gospel everywhere, who have great and proper influence, it is not the paraphernalia of their profession, but it is the man inside of all these things that is the power. And ennobled manhood is coming into a position of influence in this world that it never had in any other period, nor in any other nation outside of our great English stock, which is the root, as the Germanic from which it sprang, of the grandest manhood that ever has been. But the stature has yet to be greater, and the power and the character are yet to be greater. Now has this alteration changed the economy of the Church, or destroyed it? The Church was never so strong as it is to-day. It is not the pastor's business any longer to go from house to house as if they were ignorant. Fathers and mothers of children have now more knowledge than, three hundred years ago, the minister himself had, and the families are the bulwarks of the Church. It may be said that the Church has protected the family, but the Church itself has had its life from the family emancipated, and made larger and nobler. Well, has it promoted morality? Yes! Of all the schools on earth where intelligence and piety dwell together, the father tongue and the mother love have been the instructors of the children. There is in these centres more of real purity, and staunch honesty, and thorough integrity, than in any other institutions upon the earth.

Has this development made any difference with theology? Yes, thank God, a great deal of difference. Theology in every age is the best account that men can give of the relations of the human family to God, and the types must be the types that society in those periods is best acquainted with. When men thought that the King was Divinely King, and that the channel of instruction to mankind came through the King, it was almost inevitable that the God should be nothing but a superhuman King, having no consideration for the individual, but only thinking about His law and about the universe and about the national life; that theology stood in the way of the people, and men were running round it or creeping over it, or running against it and knocking their brains out. Well, what has the education of the common people done in that regard? It has taught men the meaning of the first words of the Lord's prayer :—" Our Father." The old theology is from the forge, from law, from government among men; the New Testament theology takes its centre in the Fatherhood of God and in the Divine love.

And how has that old governmental theology been changed? If there be one thing which the family can teach men it is the doctrine of love, and if there be one priestess that can teach it above all others it is the mother. Hers are the sufferings that precede the child's existence; through the doors and pangs of the mother it comes to life. She is the food of the child, she watches it. If it is sick she is the nurse; if it suffers she suffers yet more. She gives up all her natural liberty, she accounts no assembly so full of pleasure, and nowhere else is her life so sweet to her as by the side of the cradle or with the babe in her lap. For this she suffered, for this she gives all her knowledge, and as it grows up step by step she feeds it, and she becomes its knowledge and its righteousness, and its justice and its sanctification; she stands for it, and out of her it lives. And when the father, even, has lost out of his ear the funeral bell when the child has gone, the mother hears it toll to the end of her life. Or, when misled and overtempted, a child in ascending years breaks away from family influence and goes down step by step to disgrace and misery, and at last is afar off, the poor child sends back word: " Oh, mother, may I come home to die?" there is no reproach, the one word that rings out like an angel's trumpet is:

" Oh, my child, come home," and the mother's knee to the returning prodigal is the most sacred place in the universe this side of the feet of Jesus Christ. If there be one single creature out of heaven or on the earth that is able to teach the theologian what is the love of God, it is the mother. And that work has but begun, and both the teacher, the preacher, and the Church are to see balmier and better days in the time to come, when at last we shall have a theology that teaches the Fatherhood of God and the brotherhood of man.

Many good men are alarmed at the inevitable changes in theology and government and the conditions of the people. They want peace. Well, you can find it in the graveyard, and that is the only place. Among living men you can find no peace. Growth means disturbance; peace in any such sense as that of no investigation, no change, means death. When men say: " If you give up the old beacons you do not know where you will land,"—I know where you will land if you do not! Do you believe in God? I do. Do you believe that He has a providence over human affairs? I do. And I believe that the Hand that has steered this vagrant world through all the dark seas and storms of the

# The Reign of the Common People

past has hold of the helm yet, and through all
seeming confusions He will guide the nations
and the people safe to the golden harbour of
the millennium.  Trust Him; love Him; and
rejoice !

## IV

## ELOQUENCE AND ORATORY[1]

I CONGRATULATE myself, always, for the privilege of appearing before a Philadelphia audience — intelligent, sympathetic, appreciative; but never more than now, when the audience is assembled both to behold, and to bear witness to, one of the noblest institutions that could be established in your midst; one of the most needed; and one which I have reason to believe has been established under the inspiration of the highest motives, not only of patriotism in education, but of religion itself. This city—eminent in many respects for its institutions, and for its various collections which make civilization so honourable—I congratulate, that now, at last, it has established a school of oratory in this central position, equidistant from the South, from the West, and from the North, as a fitting centre from which should go out influences that shall exalt, if not regenerate, public senti-

[1]Originally delivered in Philadelphia, in the year 1876, at the opening of the School of Oratory.

ment on the subject of oratory; for, while progress has been made, and is making, in the training of men for public speaking, I think I may say that, relative to the exertions that are put forth in other departments of education, this subject is behind almost all others. Training in this department is the great want of our day; for we are living in a land whose genius, whose history, whose institutions, whose people, eminently demand oratory. There is nothing that draws men more quickly to any centre than the hope of hearing important subjects wisely discussed with full fervour of manhood; and that is oratory—truth bearing upon conduct, and character set home by the living force of the full man. And nowhere, in the field, in the forum, in the pulpit, or in schools, is there found to be a living voice that informs of beauty, traces rugged truth, and gives force and energy to its utterance, that people do not crowd and throng there.

We have demonstrations enough, fortunately, to show that truth alone is not sufficient; for truth is the arrow, but man is the bow that sends it home. There be many men who are the light of the pulpit, whose thought is profound, whose learning is universal, but whose

offices are unspeakably dull. They do make
known the truth; but without fervour, without
grace, without beauty, without inspiration; and
discourse upon discourse would fitly be called
*the funeral of important subjects !*

Nowhere else is there to be so large a disclosure of what is possible from man acting
upon men, as in oratory. In ancient times,
and in other lands, circumstances more or less
propitious developed the force of eloquence in
special instances, or among particular classes.
But consider the nature of our own institutions.
Consider that nothing can live in our midst until it has accepted its mission of service to the
whole people.

Now and then, men, mistaking good sense,
speak contemptuously of popularizing learning, and of popularizing science; but popular
intelligence is that atmosphere in which all
high scientific truth and research, and all
learning, in its amplest extent, are, by advance
in civilization, to find their nourishment and
stimulation; and throughout our land the people demand to know what are the principles
of government, what is the procedure of
courts, what is the best thought in regard to
national policy, what are the ripening thoughts
respecting the reformations of the times, what

is social truth, what is civil truth, and what is divine truth. These things are discussed in the cabin, in the field, in the court-house, in the legislative hall, everywhere, throughout forty or fifty millions of people. This is in accordance with the nature of our institutions and our customs ; and to the living voice more largely than to any other source are we indebted for the popularization of learning and knowledge, and for motive force, which the printed page can scarcely give in any adequate measure.

Yet, though this is in accordance with the necessity of our times, our institutions and our customs, I think that oratory, with the exception of here and there an instance which is supposed to be natural, is looked upon, if not with contempt, at least with discredit, as a thing artificial ; as a mere science of ornamentation ; as a method fit for actors who are not supposed to express their own sentiments, but unfit for a living man who has earnestness and sincerity and purpose.

Still, on the other hand, I hold that oratory has this test and mark of divine providence, in that God, when He makes things perfect, signifies that He is done by throwing over them the robe of beauty ; for beauty is the divine thought of excellence. All things, growing in their earlier stages, are rude. All of them are in vigorous strength, it may be; but not until the blossom comes, and the fruit hangs pendant, has the vine evinced for what it was made. God is a God of beauty; and beauty is everywhere the final process. When things have come to that, they have touched their limit.

Now a living force that brings to itself all the resources of imagination, all the inspirations of feeling, all that is influential in body, in voice, in eye, in gesture, in posture, in the whole animated man, is in strict analogy with the divine thought and the divine arrangement; and there is no misconstruction more utterly untrue and fatal than this: that oratory is an artificial thing, which deals with baubles and trifles, for the sake of making bubbles of pleasure for transient effect on mercurial audiences. So far from that, it is the consecration of the whole man to the noblest purposes to which one can address himself—the education and inspiration of his fellow men by all that there is in learning, by all that there is in thought, by all that there is in feeling, by all that there is in all of them, sent home through the channels of taste and of beauty. And so regarded, oratory should take its place among the highest departments of education.

I have said that it is disregarded largely; so it is; and one of the fruits of this disregard is that men fill all the places of power—how? With force misdirected; with energy not half so fruitful as it might be; with sincerity that knows not how to spread its wings and fly. I think that if you were to trace and to analyze the methods which prevail in all the departments of society, you would find in no other such contempt of culture, and in no other such punishment of this contempt.

May I speak of my own profession, from a lifelong acquaintance—from now forty years of public life and knowledge and observation? May I say, without being supposed to arrogate anything to my own profession, that I know of no nobler body of men, of more various accomplishments, of more honesty, of more self-sacrifice, and of more sincerity, than the clergymen of America? And yet, with exceptional cases, here and there, I cannot say that the profession represents eminence : I mean eminence, not in eloquence, but in oratory. I bear them witness that they mean well; I bear them witness that in multitudes of cases they are grotesque; that in multitudes of other cases they are awkward; and that in multitudes still greater they are dull. They are living witnesses to show how much can be done by men that are in earnest without offices, and without the adjuvants of imagination and of taste, by training; and they are living witnesses also, I think, of how much is left undone to make truth palatable, and to make men eager to hear it and earnest to receive it, by the lack of that very training which they have despised—or at any rate neglected.

Or, shall I ask you to scrutinize the manner and the methods that prevail in our courts— the everlasting monotone and seesaw? Shall I ask you to look at the intensity that raises itself to the highest pitch in the beginning, and that then, running in a screaming monotone, wearies, if it does not affright, all that hear it?

Or, shall I ask you to consider the wild way in which speaking takes place in our political conflicts throughout the country—the bellowing of one, the shouting of another, the grotesqueness of a third, and the want of any given method, or any controlled emotion, in almost all of them.

How much squandering there is of the voice! How little is there of the advantage that may come from conversational tones! How seldom does a man dare to acquit himself with pathos and fervour! And the men are themselves mechanical, and methodical in the bad way, who are most afraid of the artificial training that is given in the schools, and who so often show by the fruit of their labour that the want of oratory is the want of education.

How remarkable is sweetness of voice in the mother, in the father, in the household! The music of no chorded instruments brought together is, for sweetness, like the music of familiar affection when spoken by brother and sister, or by father and mother.

Conversation itself belongs to oratory. Where is there a wider, a more ample field for the impartation of pleasure or knowledge than at a festive dinner? But how often do we find that when men, having well eaten and drunken, arise to speak, they are well qualified to keep silence and utterly disqualified to speak! How rare it is to find felicity of diction on such occasions! How seldom do we see men who are educated to a fine sense of what is fit and proper at gatherings of this kind! How many men there are who are weighty in argument, who have abundant resources, and who are almost boundless in their power at other times and in other places, but who when in company among their kind are exceedingly unapt in their methods! Having none of the secret instruments by which the elements of nature may be touched, having no skill and no power in this direction, they stand as machines before living, sensitive men. A man may be as a master before an instrument; only the instrument is dead, while he has the living hand; and out of that dead instrument what wondrous harmony springs forth at his touch! And if you can electrify an audience by the power of a living man on dead things, how much more should that audience be electrified when the chords are living and the man is alive, and he knows how to touch them with divine inspiration!

I advocate, therefore, in its full extent, and for every reason of humanity, of patriotism, and of religion, a more thorough culture of oratory; and I define oratory to be *the art of influencing conduct with the truth set home by all the resources of the living man.* Its aim is not to please men, but to build them up; and the pleasure which it imparts is one of the methods by which it seeks to do this. It aims to get access to men by allaying their prejudices. A person who, with unwelcome truths, undertakes to carry them to men who do not

wish them, but who need them, undertakes a
task which is like drawing near to a fortress.
The times have gone by, but you remember
them, when, if I had spoken here on certain
themes belonging to patriotism which now are
our glory, I should have stood before you as
before so many castles locked and barred.
How unwelcome was the truth! But if one
had the art of making the truth beautiful; if
one had the art of coaxing the keeper of the
gate to turn the key and let the interloping
thought come in; if one could by persuasion
control the Cerberus of hatred, of anger, of
envy, of jealousy, that sits at the gate of men's
souls, and watches against unwelcome truths;
if one could by eloquence give sops to this
monster, and overcome him, would it not be
worth while to do it? Are we to go on still
cudgelling, and cudgelling, and cudgelling
men's ears with coarse processes? Are we to
consider it a special providence when any good
comes from our preaching or our teaching?
Are we never to study how skillfully to pick the
lock of curiosity, to unfasten the door of fancy,
to throw wide open the halls of emotion, and
to kindle the light of inspiration in the souls
of men? Is there any reality in oratory? It
is all real!

First, in the orator is the man. Let no man who is a sneak try to be an orator. The method is not the substance of oratory. A man who is to be an orator must have something to say. He must have something that in his very soul he feels to be worth saying. He must have in his nature that kindly sympathy which connects him with his fellow men, and which so makes him a part of the audience which he moves that his smile is their smile, that his tear is their tear, and that the throb of his heart becomes the throb of the hearts of the whole assembly. A man that is humane, a lover of his kind, full of all earnest and sweet sympathy for their welfare, has in him the original element, the substance of oratory, which is truth. But in this world truth needs nursing and helping; it needs every advantage; for the underflow of life is animal, and the channels of human society have been taken possession of by lower influences beforehand. The devil squatted on human territory before the angel came to dispossess him. Pride and intolerance, arrogance and its cruelty, selfishness and its greed, all the lower appetites and passions, do swarm, and do hold in thrall the under-man that each one of us yet carries— the man of flesh, on which the spirit-man seeks to ride, and by which too often he is thrown and trampled under foot. The truth in its attempt to wean the better from the worse needs every auxiliary and every adjuvant.

Therefore, the man who goes forth to speak the truth, whether men will hear or whether they will forbear, and goes with the determination that they *shall* hear; the man who carries victory in his hope; the man who has ir-refragable courage—it is not enough that he has in his soul this element, which, though it be despised, is the foundation element, and which comes first by birth, thanks to your father and mother, thanks to the providence that gave you such a father and such a mother, and thanks to the God who inspires it and sanctifies it. With this predisposition and this substance of truth which men need, and which is to refashion human life in all its parts, the question arises whether there is need of any-thing more than gracious culture. Well, so long as men are in the body they need the body. There are some who think they have well-nigh crucified the body. If they have, why are they lingering here below, where they are not useful, and where they are not needed? So long as men touch the ground, and feel their own weight, so long they need the aptitudes and the instrumentalities of the human body; and one of the very first steps in oratory is that which trains the body to be the welcome and glad servant of the soul— which it is not always; for many and many a one who has acres of thought has little bodily culture, and as little grace of manner; and many and many a one who has sweetening inside has cacophony when he speaks. Harsh, rude, hard, bruising, are his words.

The first work, therefore, is to teach a man's body to serve his soul; and in this work the education of the bodily presence is the very first step. We had almost extinguished the power of the human body by our pulpits, which, in early days, were the sources and centres of popular eloquence such as there was; for men followed the Apocalyptic figure of the candlestick, the pulpit in the church representing the candlestick, and the minister being supposed to be the light in it. In those days of symbolization everything had to be symbolized; and when a church was built they made a pulpit that was like the socket of a candlestick, and put a man into it; and thus entubbed he looked down afar upon his congregation to speak unto them! Now, what man could win a coy and proud companion if he were obliged to court at fifty feet distance from her? or, what man, pleading for his life, would plead afar off, as through a speaking trumpet, from the second story, to one down below?

Nay, men have been covered up. The introduction of platforms has been thought, on the whole, to be a somewhat discourteous thing. I will tell you, if you will indulge me, a little reminiscence of my own experience. In the church where I minister there was no pulpit; there was only a platform; and some of the elect ladies, honourable and precious, waited upon me to know if I would not permit a silk screen to be drawn across the front of my table, so that my legs and feet need not be seen. My reply to them was, " I will, on one condition—that whenever I make a pastoral call at your houses you will have a green silk bag into which I may put my legs."

If the legs and feet are tolerable in a parlour, or in a social room, why are they not tolerable on a platform? It takes the whole man to make a man; and at times there are no gestures that are comparable to the simple stature of the man himself. So it behooves us to train men to use the whole of themselves. Frequently the foot is emphasis, and the posture is oftentimes power, after a word, or accompanying a word; and men learn to perceive the thought coming afar off from the man himself who foreshadows it by his action.

You shall no longer, when men are obliged to stand disclosed before the whole audience, see ministers bent over a desk, like a weary horse crooked over a hitching block, and preaching first on one leg, and then on the other. To be a gentleman in the presence of an audience is one of the first lessons which oratory will teach the young aspiring speaker.

But, beside that, what power there is in posture, or in gesture! By it, how many discriminations are made; how many smooth things are rolled off; how many complex things men are made to comprehend! How many things the body can tongue when the tongue itself cannot well utter the thing desired! The tongue and the person are to coöperate; and having been trained to work together, their result is spontaneous, unthought of, unarranged for.

Now, to the real natural man—and the natural man is the educated man; not the thing from which he sprang—how much is to be added! Many a man will hear the truth for the pleasure of hearing it, who would not hear it for the profit of hearing it; and so there must be something more than its plain statement. Among other things, the voice—perhaps the most important of all, and the least cultured—should not be forgotten. How many men are there that can speak from day to day one hour, two hours, three hours, without exhaustion, and without hoarseness? But it is in the power of the vocal organs, and of the ordinary vocal organs, to do this. What multitudes of men weary themselves out because they put their voice on a hard run at the top of its compass!—and there is no relief to them, and none, unfortunately, to the audience. But the voice is like an orchestra. It ranges high up, and can shriek betimes like the scream of an eagle; or it is low as a lion's tone; and at every intermediate point is some peculiar quality. It has in it the mother's whisper and the father's command. It has in it warning and alarm. It has in it sweetness. It is full of mirth and full of gayety. It glitters, though it is not seen with all its sparkling fancies. It ranges high, intermediate, or low, in obedience to the will, unconsciously to him who uses it; and men listen through the long hour, wondering that it is so short, and quite unaware that they have been bewitched out of their weariness by the charm of a voice, not artificial, not pre-arranged at the time in the man's thought, but by assiduous training made to be his second nature. Such a voice answers to the soul, and is its beating.

Now against this training manifold objections are made. It is said that it is unworthy of manhood that men should be so trained. The conception of a man is that of blunt earnestness. It is said that if a man knows what he wants to say, he can say it; that if he knows what he wants to have men do, the way is for him to pitch at them. That seems to be about the idea which ordinarily prevails on this subject. Shoot a man, as you would a rocket in war; throw him as you would a hand-grenade; and afterwards, if you please, look to see where he hits; and woe be to those who touch the fragments! Such appears to be the notion which many have on this subject. But where else, in what other relation, does a man so reason? Here is the highest function to which any man can address himself—the attempt to vitalize men; to give warmth to frigid natures; to give aspirations to the dull and low-flying; to give purpose to conduct, and to evolve character from con-

duct; to bring to bear every part of one's self
—the thinking power; the perceptive power;
the intuitions; the imagination; all the sweet
and overflowing emotions. The grace of the
body; its emphasis; its discriminations; the
power of the eye and of the voice—all these
belong to the blessedness of this work.

" No," says the man of the school of the
beetle, " buzz, and fight, and hit where you
can." Thus men disdain this culture as
though it were something effeminate; as
though it were a science of ornamentation;
as though it were a means of stealing men's
convictions, not enforcing them; and as
though it lacked calibre and dignity.

But why should not this reasoning be applied to everything else? The very man who
will not train his own voice to preach, to
lecture, to discourse, whether in the field or
in the legislative hall or in the church, will
pay large dues through weary quarters to drill
his daughter's voice to sing hymns, and canzo-
nets, and other music. This is not counted
to be unworthy of the dignity of womanhood.

" But," it is said, " does not the voice come
by nature? " Yes; but is there anything that
comes by nature which stays as it comes if it
is worthily handled? We receive one talent

that we may make it five ; and we receive five talents that we may make them ten. There is no one thing in man that he has in perfection till he has it by culture. We know that in respect to everything but the voice in speech. Is not the ear trained to acute hearing ? Is not the eye trained in science ? Do men not school the eye, and make it quick-seeing by patient use ? Is a man, because he has learned a trade, and was not born with it, thought to be less a man ? Because we have made discoveries of science and adapted them to manufacture ; because we have developed knowledge by training, are we thought to be unmanly ? Shall we, because we have un-folded our powers by the use of ourselves for that noblest of purposes, the inspiration and elevation of mankind, be less esteemed ? Is the school of human training to be disdained when by it we are rendered more useful to our fellow men ?

But it is said that this culture is artificial ; that it is mere posturing ; that it is simple ornamentation. Ah ! that is not because there has been so much of it, but because there has been so little of it. If a man were to begin, as he should, early ; or if, beginning late, he were to addict himself assiduously to it, then the graces of speech, the graces of oratory, would be to him what all learning must be before it is perfect, namely, spontaneous. If he were to be trained earlier, then his training would not be called the science of ostentation or of acting.

Never is a man thoroughly taught until he has forgotten how he learned. Do you remember when you tottered from chair to chair? Now you walk without thinking that you learned to walk. Do you remember when your inept hands wandered through the air towards the candle, or towards the mother's bosom? Now how regulated, how true to your wish, how quick, how sharp to the touch, are those hands! But it was by learning that they became so far perfected. Their perfection is the fruit of training.

Let one think of what he is doing, and he does it ill. If you go into your parlour, where your wife and children are, you always know what to do with yourself—or almost always! You are not awkward in your postures, nor are you awkward with your hands; but let it be understood that there are a dozen strangers to be present, and you begin to think how to appear well before them; and the result of your thinking about it is that you appear very ill. Where to put your hands, and where to put yourself, you do not know; how to stand or how to sit troubles you; whether to hold up one hand or the other hand, or to hold both down, or both up, is a matter of thought with you.

Let me walk on the narrowest of these boards upon which I stand, and I walk with simplicity and perfect safety, because I scarcely think of walking; but lift that board fifty feet above the ground, and let me walk on it as far as across this building, and let me think of the consequences that would result if I were to fall, and how I would tremble and reel! The moment a man's attention is directed to that which he does, he does it ill. When the thing which a man does is so completely mastered that there is an absence of volition, and he does it without knowing it, he does it easily; but when the volition is not subdued, and when, therefore, he does not act spontaneously, he is conscious of what he does, and the consciousness prevents his doing it easily. Unconsciousness is indispensable to the doing a thing easily and well.

Now, in regard to the training of the orator, it should begin in boyhood, and should be part and parcel of the lessons of the school. Grace;

posture; force of manner; the training of the eye, that it may look at men, and pierce them, and smile upon them, and bring summer to them, and call down storms and winter upon them; the development of the hand, that it may wield the sceptre, or beckon with sweet persuasion—these things do not come artificially; they belong to man. Why, men think that nature means that which lies back of culture. Then you ought never to have departed from babyhood; for that is the only nature you had to begin with. But is nature the acorn forever? Is not the oak nature? Is not that which comes from the seed the best representation of the divine conception of the seed? And as men we are seeds. Culture is but planting them and training them according to their several natures; and nowhere is training nobler than in preparing the orator for the great work to which he educates himself—the elevation of his kind, through truth, through earnestness, through beauty, through every divine influence.

But it is said that the times are changing, and that we ought not to attempt to meddle with that which God has provided for. Say men, "The truth is before you; there is your Bible; go preach the Word of God." Well, if you are not to meddle with what God has provided for, why was not the Bible sent instead of you? You were sent because the very object of a preacher was to give the truth a living form, and not have it lie in the dead letter. As to its simplicity and as to its beauty, I confute you with your own doctrine; for, as I read the sacred text, it is, "Adorn the doctrine of God our Saviour." We are to make it beautiful. There are times when we cannot do it. There are times for the scalpel, there are times for the sword, and there are times for the battle-axe; but these are exceptional. "Let every one of us please his neighbour for his good to edification" is a standing command; and we are to take the truth, of every kind, and if possible bring it in its summer guise to men.

But it is said, "Our greatest orators have not been trained." How do you know? It may be that Patrick Henry went crying in the wilderness of poor speakers, without any great training; I will admit that now and then there are gifts so eminent and so impetuous that they break through ordinary necessities; but even Patrick Henry was eloquent only under great pressure; and there remain the results of only one or two of his efforts. Daniel Webster is supposed in many respects to have been the greatest American orator of his time; but there never lived a man who was so studious of everything he did, even to the buttons on his coat, as Daniel Webster. Henry Clay was prominent as an orator, but though he was not a man of the schools, he was a man who schooled himself; and by his own thought and taste and sense of that which was fitting and beautiful, he became, through culture, an accomplished orator.

If you go from our land to other lands; if you go to the land which has been irradiated by parliamentary eloquence; if you go to the people of Great Britain; if you go to the great men in ancient times who lived in the intellect; if you go to the illustrious names that every one recalls—Demosthenes and Cicero—they represent a life of work.

Not until Michael Angelo had been the servant and the slave of matter did he learn to control matter; and not until he had drilled and drilled and drilled himself were his touches free and easy as the breath of summer, and full of colour as the summer itself. Not until Raphael had subdued himself by colour was he the crowning artist of beauty. You shall not find one great sculptor, nor one great architect, nor one great painter, nor one eminent man in any department of art, nor one great scholar, nor one great statesman, nor one divine of universal gifts, whose greatness, if you inquire, you will not find to be the fruit of study, and of the evolution that comes from study.

It is said, furthermore, that oratory is one of the lost arts. I have heard it said that our struggles brought forth not one prominent orator. This fact reveals a law which has been overlooked—namely, that aristocracy diminishes the number of great men, and makes the few so much greater than the average that they stand up like the pyramids in the deserts of Egypt; whereas, democracy distributes the resources of society, and brings up the whole mass of the people; so that under a democratic government great men never stand so high above the average as they do when society has a level far below them. Let building go up on building around about the tallest spire in this city, and you dwarf the spire, though it stand as high as heaven, because everything by which it is surrounded has risen higher.

Now throughout our whole land there was more eloquence during our struggles than there was previously; but it was in far more mouths. It was distributed. There was in the mass of men a higher method of speaking, a greater power in addressing their fellow men; and though single men were not so prominent as they would have been under other circumstances, the reason is one for which we should be grateful. There were more men at a higher average, though there were fewer men at an extreme altitude.

Then it is said that books, and especially newspapers, are to take the place of the living voice. Never! never! The miracle of modern times, in one respect, is the Press; to it is given a wide field and a wonderful work; and when it shall be clothed with all the moral inspirations, with all the ineffable graces, that come from simplicity and honesty and conviction, it will have a work second almost to none other in the land. Like the light, it carries knowledge every day around the globe. What is done at St. Paul's in the morning is known, or ever half the day has run around, in Wall Street, New York. What is done in New York at the rising of the sun is, before the noontide hour, known in California. By the power of the wire, and of the swift-following engine, the papers spread at large vast quantities of information before myriad readers throughout the country; but the office of the papers is simply to convey information. They cannot plant it. They cannot open the soil and put it into the furrow. They cannot enforce it. It is given only to the living man, standing before men with the seed of knowledge in his hand, to open the furrows in the living souls of men, and sow the seed, and cover the furrows again. Not until human nature is other than it is, will the function of the living voice—the greatest force on earth among men—cease. Not until then will the orator be useless, who brings to his aid all that is fervid in feeling; who incarnates in himself the truth; who is for the hour the living reason, as well as the reasoner; who is for the moment the moral sense; who carries in himself the importunity and the urgency of zeal; who brings his influence to bear upon men in various ways; who adapts himself continually to the changing conditions of the men that are before him; who plies them by softness and by hardness, by light and by darkness, by hope and by fear; who stimulates them or represses them at his will. Nor is there, let me say, on God's footstool, anything so crowned and so regal as the sensation of one who faces an audience in a worthy cause, and with amplitude of means, and defies them, fights them, controls them, *conquers* them.

Great is the advance of civilization; mighty are the engines of force, but man is greater than that which he produces. Vast is that machine which stands in the dark unconsciously lifting, lifting—the only humane slave—the iron slave—the Corliss engine; but he that made the engine is greater than the engine itself. Wonderful is the skill by which that most exquisite mechanism of modern life, the watch, is constructed; but greater is the man that made the watch than the watch that is made. Great is the Press, great are the hundred instrumentalities and institutions and customs of society; but above them all is Man. The living force is greater than any of its creations—greater than society, greater than its laws. "The Sabbath was made for man, and not man for the Sabbath," saith the Lord. Man is greater than his own institutions. And this living force is worthy of all culture—of all culture in the power of beauty; of all culture in the direction of persuasion; of all culture in the art of reasoning.

To make men patriots, to make men Christians, to make men the sons of God, let all the doors of heaven be opened, and let God drop down charmed gifts—winged imagination, all-perceiving vision, and all-judging reason. Whatever there is that can make men wiser and better—let it descend upon the head of him who has consecrated himself to the work of mankind, and who has made himself an orator for man's sake and for God's sake.

## V

## WILLIAM ELLERY CHANNING[1]

I DO not propose to speak to-night at any length. It is now a time at which Dr. Channing would have been abed and asleep for an hour. You have had a banquet, if ever an audience had; and you have also had the benediction of a good sound orthodox clergyman at the end of it. And it seems to me that the consent of men, whether they are in the Mother Church or in any of the scattered sectarian churches,—orthodox, half-orthodox, or heterodox,—is all gained to-night, and gained on one point : that a man who loves God fervently and his fellow men heartily, and devotes his life to that love, is a member of every communion and of every church, and is orthodox in spite of orthodoxy or anything else !

There is one point, however, that has been pressed upon my mind, as I have been overwhelmed with the richness of the thoughts and

[1] At a celebration of the centenary anniversary of Channing's birth, held in Boston, April 7, 1880.

illustrations of the speakers gone by. So warm and enthusiastic have been the eulogies to-night, that one might almost imagine that Dr. Channing was himself the light of the world! But no; so rich is God, so all-pervading, so incarnated in every soul that thinks and in every heart that throbs, that Dr. Channing was but one single taper shining in the darkness of this world, and drawing his light from the great solar Fountain, God. He was the mouthpiece of his time; but his time had prepared the material which he expressed. No man, in any age, though he stand head and shoulders above his fellows, is competent to do much more than has been wrought out for him,—to be the teacher of those things which have been made needed, and manifestly needed, by the experience of millions of men, and to give intellectual expression to those truths which in their emotive form have welled up in thousands and tens of thousands of bosoms. Dr. Channing felt all the accumulated force, moral and social, of the times gone by and the times at hand in which he lived. And so, though he was great, mankind behind him was greater, the time was greater, and the all-informing spirit of God was greater yet.

In my boyhood, I went to Boston in 1826,

and was thrown into the very centre and heat of that great controversy which was raging, in which my father was an eloquent thunderer on one side, and in which Dr. Channing was an eloquent silent man on the other side. Mostly his work had been done, at that time. Do I not remember the image of that day? In my own nature enthusiastic, sincere, and truthful, did not what my father thought become what I thought? And did I not know that Unitarians were the children of the devil? And did I not know that those heresiarchs, if they had not fallen from heaven, ought to fall from the earth? And did I not regard Channing, I will not say as a man misled, but as a man demented, in whom was the spirit of error, leading men down to perdition, and who ought to be silenced, and all of whose followers ought to be scourged? Did I not read in those days the haughty statement, the reply, the rejoinder, and then the diffusive controversy generally?

And yet time has wrought with me, as it has wrought with you, and with all men, wonderful changes; and now those two men, my father and Dr. Channing, that stood over against each other,—to my young seeming,— as wide apart as the East from the West, I see standing together, and travelling in precisely the same lines, and towards precisely the same results. For did not Lyman Beecher feel that, as the doctrine of God and of moral government was presented in the day in which he lived, the glory of God was obscured, that men were bound hand and foot, and that the sweetness and the beauty of the love of Christ in the Gospel were misunderstood, or even veiled and utterly hidden? And what was he striving for but such a renovation of the old orthodoxy as should let the light of the glory of God, as it shone in the face of Jesus Christ, have a fair chance at folks? And what was Channing striving for? He felt that the old formulas and statements of men did not let out the whole circumference, nor did it give the whole force and beauty of the character of God. He, too, was driving, as best he could, the clouds out of heaven, and seeking to make the character of God more resplendent, and morally more effective to mankind. And there they stood bombarding each other, both of them with the same grand object and motive; like two valiant men-of-war, that are giving each other broadside after broadside, and yet are on a stream of Providence that is carrying them unconsciously in the same direction! They sailed side by side, and as they met in heaven I think they lifted up hands of wonder and exclaimed, " Is it possible that I am here—and you ? "

My estimate of Channing is not less because my estimate of the whole force of society is greater. He was *one* of the men, and but one, —a great and noble and leading man. Ten thousand other things were working. When Sisera was at his battle, the stars in their courses, it is said, fought against him ; and, when God hath great work on hand, the stars, and everything that is beneath them, are working in one direction. The changes in governments, the advance in laws, the development of a better political economy, the evolution of commonwealths, the progress of science and of the mechanic arts, but especially the science of mind, are working out a final theology by working to the same great end,—the emancipation of man, the clarity of his understanding, the sovereignty of his conscience, the sympathies of his soul, and the full disclosure of God, over all, blessed forever. And it is enough glory to say of Channing that he understood the day in which he lived, and understood that he was appointed to be a pilot to the times that were to come after ; and that whatever he did administratively he did intelligently, that the young and the vital wood that carried the sap and the life of the tree might have a chance.

Those who are horticulturists will understand that the bark that carried the sap last year will have to get out of the way, and let the bark that comes on this year have a chance; and the kind pomologist, with his knife, often slits the bark of the cherry tree that is conservative, to give a chance to that which has a hereditary right to be the bark, and let the bark-bound diameter of the tree expand a little. Dr. Channing, among other men, used the knife for the sake of letting the new truth, which was struggling for a larger diameter in the world, have a chance.

Well, what has been the result? That was one hundred years ago to-day. And what would Channing think if he were allowed to stand here to-night? He would have been half deaf by this time, if he had heard everything that has been said on this platform; but, if he turned his eye upwards, and saw the change that has come over the American world, to say nothing of Christendom, during the last hundred years, and contrasted the spirit of antipathy which existed between sect and sect, between theologian and theologian, and the spirit which exists between them now, what would be his thought ? Even so sympathetic a man as my father never saw an Arminian come into his church in that early day, that he did not feel bound to give him such a dose of Calvinism as would physic him for a year ! I know very well how stringent were the habits, the methods, the peculiarities of each sect, and how each sect defended itself. They were like so many nests of wasps in neighbouring trees, each one stinging for his own nest, and each one fighting against the nest of every other.

So the fiery sects, if they were not dead and buried in worldliness, or when they revived and came to life, were animated by a spirit of antipathy and suspicion and jealousy. Of course the spirit of envy and jealousy is universal and continuous ; but in that early day there was the spirit of criticism and of suspicion, and it all sprang from a very obvious source. For had they not embraced that world-wide heresy, that God had committed His kingdoms in this world to the consciences of His official disciples, and had ordained their consciences to govern the consciences of all mankind? Has it not been the bane of every sect, from the beginning to this day, that men have felt that they were the special depositaries of divine knowledge, and that the deposition gave them the power to dictate to other men what they should think and what they should believe, and to hold the rod of everlasting damnation over their head, if they did not think and believe as they were told? All men held substantially this view then, and some men hold it even now. So it came to pass that each sect followed its own notion of God, marking out exactly the line of the wall, throwing up exactly the right bulwarks, and defending what each man knew to be the one exclusive truth of creation, and feeling bound to look sharp at all the others, to contest them, and to condemn them, that the deposit of truth which each one had in purity might have a fair chance in this world!

That is all changed. I remember when you could not get a minister of the Episcopal Church, and of the Unitarian, and of the Universalist, and the Swedenborgian, and of the Baptist, and of the Congregationalist, on to a common platform. You could scarcely do it on the Fourth of July, and it was a wonder then that they did not fight. But, to-day, on how many different subjects are they glad to come together and consult! And how marvellous an event is it of the time in which we live, to see all these staunch churches, by their staunchest ministers and advocates, stand together through one long day with nothing on their tongue but praises of that heretic Unitarian, Dr. William Ellery Channing! Time and the world *do* move. Changes *have* been wrought!

And more than that: there has come in, from influences which it has pleased God to give forth, and distribute in the heart and understanding of many a man, but by none more than by Channing, a change by which it is understood in this world that, if God is to have all the glory, then He must be represented to be a God that is altogether glorious; that, if He is to have sovereign and absolute control of men, then He is to have it because all the faculties of the human soul which He infixed in mankind for the very purpose of judging what is right and what is wrong, what is just and what is unjust, what is holy and pure and what is unholy and impure, are satisfied with the representations that are made of Him; and the whole Christian world to-day is feeling after such a representation of God as mankind will not let die out. No view of

God will be allowed to reign which does not conform to the enlightened moral sense of good men. While there are men who are atheists largely because the God on which they have been fed is not God, is a misrepresentation of the true God, in churches all over our land,—and, with perhaps more reluctant step, in the churches of other lands,—the cry of Christendom is: "Give to us a God that shall not be apologized for! Give to us a God that we do not need to defend! Give to us a God that, when the child, and the mother of the child, and the just man, and the loving soul, look up, they shall say, ' Whom have I in heaven but Thee? and there is none that I desire upon earth beside Thee.' "

The Calvinistic theology of New England before Channing's day had become intolerable to the best Orthodox men, and Channing was but one of many who sought its modification. Judged by the Scotch, the Genevese standard —many noble men, Edwards, Hopkins, Bellamy, West, Spring, Backus, Strong, Dwight, and a host of others, were smoothing its features, and softening its immedicable harshness. The revolt against this system of organized Fatalism and Infinite Despotism is not yet ended. In the lecture-rooms of the schools, where intellect has supreme sway and heart is excluded, the system lives, but in the pulpit it has perished. The educated moral sense of the laymen has slain it. The free air of human life, the play of Christian sympathies upon it, have made the employment of it as impossible as to uphold astrology, or alchemy, or the inquisition.

But, while we thus speak of Calvinism, John Calvin was illustrious as a radical. He broke away from the reigning spirit of his own times, and led the spirit of free inquiry. Were he alive in our day, no man would scourge Calvinism with such resounding blows as John Calvin! Nor was his theological system without great benefit, in an age when the king and the priest had more power than God upon the senses and the imagination. Men believed in nothing that they could not see and handle. The Church was busy in bringing all high and ineffable truth into a sensuous condition.

Over against this magnificent Rome, with its cathedrals, altars, robed priests, processions, gorgeous ceremonies, filling the eye, and bringing down the spiritual man to the bondage of the senses, Calvin wrought out a theology of thought, logical, elaborate, complete. When men pointed to the visible

Church, its flowing rituals and its impressive trappings, and asked tauntingly, "Where is your religion? There is ours, visible to all men, sublime and beautiful," Calvin pointed to his system, invisible yet powerful, addressed to reason, not sense; a system that aroused fear, that developed imagination, that moved in men's thoughts as laws of nature move upon the earth. His God was full-orbed in power, and His light and glory extinguished the false lights of the throne and the altar. It was a time when nations were being dashed in pieces as a potter's vessel; and Calvin's God was the very divine iconoclast, going forth to overthrow idols and polluted temples, and drive headlong all usurpers of His prerogatives. His attributes as expounded by Calvin did not shock the rude ideas of that day. They only concentred in God the barbaric authority to which men had wearily and long submitted in magistrates and masters. Better one despot than a thousand. That system, which now oppresses the conscience and shocks the moral sense, in its day emancipated reason, developed the moral sense, and inspired men with ideas that led to liberty in the State and in the Church.

But, like the steel armour of our fathers, admirable in its day, it can be no longer worn. The spirit of God has advanced men beyond the need of such an instrument. It must be placed in the hall, or gathered in military museums, with broadswords, spears, culverins, and the whole panoply of antiquated weapons.

Our age has witnessed and is still rejoicing in a better idea of *justice*. There has been a great advance in our day in the conception of justice, as an emanation of sympathy and love, and not a deification of combativeness and destructiveness. Justice has formerly been made vindictive rather than vindicatory. The principle of hate has ruled in civil law, in government, in theology, and in the churches. We have had a fighting, not a loving Christianity. Repulsion has been stronger than attraction, dislike than sympathy. Upon this dreary winter, spring is advancing. It has not yet conquered. Here and there come blustering days, to renew the rigour and to destroy this new life. But the Sun of Righteousness is now high in the heavens. The days are longer; the light advances, and the warmth. All things are tending to draw men to each other. The things in which men agree are increasingly more important than those in which they differ. Love is growing, hate is weakening.

More than that, I think in the past one hundred years—and this, the birthday of Channing, marks the beginning of it—there has not only been a change in the spirit of sects, in the notions of government and in theology, but there has also been a wonderful progress in true religion. If you measure religion by the exact forms of any of the highly organized churches,—our mother, Rome, and her eldest daughter, the Episcopal Church; if you measure it by dogma and formality and ordinance, in the different aspects in which the denominations present it; if you measure its condition by the Westminster Catechism, or by the Confession of Faith, or by any of the mediæval Confessions, or by the hitherto standing claims of any of the organized religious bodies,—I think it must be admitted that there is a decadence of religion. But how? When the morning star begins to shine, the nimble lamplighters of our cities go around extinguishing one gaslight after another. They were substitutes for daylight; but, when the sun is coming up, there is no longer use for gaslight.

# William Ellery Channing

And shall any man say, " They are putting out the light of the world"? They are putting out the artificial lights that help us through the night, but are they destroying daylight?

If religion means veneration, there is not so much as there was. Our own institutions do not tend to breed veneration. Our children at fifteen years of age know as much as we do, and govern us at twenty! Our magistrates have but little dignity. We put them up merely that we may pelt them. To nominate a man for office in our land is to stigmatize him; and to elect him is to damn him! There is nothing old in America but trees; and people do not care for them. For it is with us as of old, when a man was accounted great as he lifted up an axe against the trees; and almost nothing in the body politic is sacred in our scrambling, active land, where men are building every one for himself. There is little veneration here; and, if that is religion, heaven help us! We have tried to breed it. We build big churches with small windows. We put out with paint what little light can get through. We have imitations of grotesque things that have come down five hundred or one thousand years, and we try to dress as they used to dress before they knew how to dress!

In every way possible, we are trying to coax the old mediæval spirit of veneration. We cannot do it; it is not bred in our day. It will not live in our land. The common school is against it; the elective franchise is against it; the whole of our society is against it. So dangerous are the lapses of men now in theology that we are all of us trying to stop that; and we are refurbishing the old armour, and the word is going out: "We must reprint the old doctrines, and we must introduce a shrewder economy in our seminaries, and we must screw up the system. It is getting loose and shackly." The engineers are screwing it up here and there, and by every means striving to make it work as it used to work. There is such a wide-spread doctrinal defection—with one or two exceptions—that, if you are to measure the progress of religion by the exact agreement of men to confession and catechism, woe be to religion!

But religion is of the heart. It is a living force. Books do not contain it, but only describe it. Creeds and catechisms may be honoured while religion is perishing; and religion may be increasing in scope and sweetness while creeds are waning. It is born in every generation, and in every heart that is a child

# William Ellery Channing

of God; and one cannot find whether men
have religion or not by bringing them to the
catechism, or by asking them how they got it.
We have learned one thing, and that is that
mankind are greater than all the governments
of mankind. We have learned that the man
is more than the church, and that the church
was made for man, and not man for the church.
We have learned that, if there is such a thing
as religion, it is not to be found in any machinery. We have learned that religion is
loving God and loving our fellow men.

Now, then, tested by that, is there more
or less religion in the age in which we live
than there was in the days that are gone by?
I say, more. I call the whole civilized world
to witness that, although there is much of the
lion, of the bear, of the eagle, and of the vul-
ture yet in mankind, and though these foul
beasts or birds float on our national banners
and represent much of the under economy of
animalism among men, yet to an extent that
was never known before in the world, there is
the spirit of sympathy of man with man disclosed. Never before has God been worshipped by the serving of His children as He
is to-day. Never before was there such an
adhesion as there is to-day to the words of

Christ, " Inasmuch as ye do it unto one of the least of these, ye do it unto Me." We worship a Christ that stands by the poor, by the slave, by the prisoner, and by the emigrant who lands, weary and discouraged, on our shores. We worship a Christ that identifies Himself with the low and the needy and the suffering. We worship a Christ that is in the hospital among the sick. If worshipping Christ is worshipping God, I am orthodox. I wish others were. I aver that Christ was never worshipped so much as He is to-day by the love, by the sympathy, and by the self-sacrificing helpfulness which we bestow upon all classes and conditions of men. Never before did the human race see a whole age and an organized nation putting their hands under the very bottom of society, and attempting to lift, not the crowned heads, not the middle classes, not the burghers and rich men, but mankind from the very lowest, taking the whole house up from its foundation. And while I see all reformatory societies attempting to reclaim men from intemperance, to cleanse our prisons, to purge out vice, to restrain all wrong; while I see the tendency everywhere to send, by showers of gold, the Gospel to benighted nations, and to promote the mission cause at home, and to educate the slave and every living creature,—shall a man stand by and tell me that religion is going down? A religion that lets these alone is no religion; and a religion by which any man or community takes care of these, and in the love of God sympathizes with man, and cares for him,—that is the true religion.

When the potato was first sent to Ireland, they planted it, and did not know where to look for the fruit. And when it blossomed and bore its little seed pods, they boiled these pods, and ate them, and did not like potatoes! If they had gone to the root of the matter, they would have liked them. They learned that later. So there are very many men who taste religion as it is shown in the pod, if I may so say; and they do not like this church, that doctrine, this ordinance, and that economy. What if you do not? These are not crops: they are merely the tools by which we try to raise crops. They are the machinery by which we work, and not the thing for which we are working. I never ate millstones; but I have eaten that which millstones have produced. And the things that grind out human love and kindness,—all may be defective; but the flour is the thing. And I say that never before was there so much holy flour as there is to-day.

There is one more thing that I think is true, and of which this celebration is significant; namely, that there is no statement of religion like religion itself. You cannot put into words the essential verities of religion. When you have used all the language that the vocabulary can give you, and tacked word to word, you cannot have made a belt that will go around the infinity and eternity of God. When by every figure that is known to fallible men, by all the sweetness of a mother's love, by all the purity of a child's love, by all the fervour of noble souls just mated, you have tried to represent God; when you have gathered up all things that are resplendent, and made them patterns of divine love,—you have done, as it were, nothing. The love of God that fills eternity, and that is marching down through eternities, bearing benison and benediction to countless spheres of existence, doubtless, besides our own,—when you attempt to put it into language and represent it by figures gathered by the limited experiences of men, it is as if you undertook to find timber for your navy in moss, and as if you undertook to decorate your cathedrals with the inconspicu-

# William Ellery Channing

ous flowers and plants that grow too small but
for the microscope. God is too big for language, too big for representation by human
experience.

The thing that most nearly represents God
is a man that is living like God. And no
man can draw that portrait or put it into
language. We can see it, and we can rejoice
in it ; but, after all, the man that is like God is
the best catechism and the best confession of
faith. And we have learned one thing,—
that, when we see such a man, he is God's,
and he is ours. " All things are yours," says
Paul. On that ground, I am as good a
Catholic as there is in this world, except the
pope and the cardinals and the bishops, and
their doctrines. And from my ownership of
every saintly woman and every saintly man
no one can hinder me. They are mine, because they are God's ; and I revere them and
love them. There is a vast amount of true
theology in the good living of the Catholic
Church. There are men that rebuke our
lukewarmness and our lives by the nobility of
theirs,—multitudes of them ; and they are all
right. Whatever the church may be that
makes them, theirs is the true theology. I
go from that into the Episcopal Church. It is

enough for me that she gave me my mother. Than that there can be no farther argument. The church that yields such blessings is not a church that I can contest, whatever her machinery may be. I ask: "What are the products? Where are the saints, men and women?" If they are Christlike, they are all right. I go into the Unitarian Church. I want no better Christians than I find there. They are orthodox, sound, by every Christian man and every Christian woman among them that makes piety beautiful in the eyes of mankind. I go into the Swedenborgian Church. Brother Ager is a good enough Christian for me. He is soundly orthodox, whatever he believes. No matter about that. I don't care what a man believes. What *is* he? That is my question. I say that what a man *is* is his confession of faith. A man's life is more important than any statement of the philosophy of that life, or of the machinery by which that life was brought into existence.

It is true that some schools are better than other schools, that some methods of teaching are very likely to be better than some others, that some statements of doctrine are better than some other statements of doctrine in their aptitude to carry men on and upward. I will not discriminate as to which I think is the better, though I can well understand that men find a difference between one and another; but this I say, that when any man has been made a Christian, luminous of heaven, he does not belong to the church that bred him: he belongs to that Church Universal which has no exposition but in the sympathies of the universe; and he belongs to you and to me. And, Mr. Chairman, don't take on airs, as if Channing was your man. He is *my* man as much as he is yours. I have seen considerable of that spirit here to-night,—and I feel bound as a Christian to fight it,—as if you had a man that you would let us come and look at, as if we might be permitted to come on this platform and worship your hero. I thank God that you have some such men to worship and to present to us. It is a sign that there is a sort of grace with you. Your doctrines may be very imperfect; but, after all, there is a grace of God that goes with imperfection. All sorts of instruments have been employed in this world. Oftentimes, too, the instrument has been more than the prophet, as when Balaam went forth on his famous ride of old. And, since all sorts of instruments are employed by the good God, no matter what the instrument is, it is the man that is created.

Here was a man, in a dark day, in a day of controversy, in a day in which men stood very differently from the way in which they stand now; and I look upon that godly man and see a lambent flame of holiness. I see that he was a light kindled in a dark place; and the sweetness of his humility strikes me. He blushes in heaven to hear what is said of him on earth, if he attends to it,—though I think likely he does not. He was a good man. If he had been in the Roman Church, he would have been a saint; and he is not less a saint, because he was in the Unitarian Church. We have learned that man is a better exposition of Christianity than doctrines, or any of the various instruments of the Church. We are learning to receive whom God receives; and whenever a man shows that he is acceptable to the Master, is wearing His spirit, and is blessed by His continual attendance, that man is sacred to us, no matter to what denomination he may belong. A man is more than doctrine,—and mankind are more than church and more than government. Next to God, the only valuable things in this universe are living men; and all nature is prepared to take care of them. God is the Fountain and Cause of all things; and all nature and all time and all providence and all grace are so many ministering servants to develop manhood in men. And the only difference there can possibly be in our view of God is this: those views of God that tend to beat men down, and to beat down their moral sense, you may be sure are false views; while the views of God that tend to lift men up, to inspire them with a holy horror of sin, to lead them to aspire to holiness, and to give them a willingness to do kindness at their own expense, to live for mankind, and if need be to shed their blood,—such views are orthodox, however defective may be the system from which they spring.

When we look back, then, one hundred years, what do we see? The greatest change, I think, that has been produced in any hundred since the Advent; and, when I look forward from this standpoint, it seems to me that we stand just about in the month of April in the history of the world, as we do in this year. We have had our dead winter, we have had our blustering, controversial month of March, and now we have our month of April, which does not know exactly whether it has left March or whether it is entering into May; but it is on the way towards summer, and soon there will come the blossoms of May already anticipated; and after that will come June, the opal of the year; and then the summer; and then the harvest. We are on the full march; and, therefore, instead of looking back to the leeks and onions of orthodoxy in Egypt, the spirit of God, the spirit of philosophy, the spirit of wisdom, the spirit of true religion, is to forget the things that are behind, and to press forward, towards the mark, for the prize of our high calling in Christ Jesus.

## VI

## CHARLES SUMNER[1]

THE best gift of God to nations is the gift of upright men—especially upright men for magistrates, statesmen, and rulers. How bountiful soever the heavens may be; how rich the earth may be in harvest; though every wind of heaven waft prosperity to its ports, till the land is crowded with warehouses stuffed to repletion with treasure, that country is poor whose citizens are not noble, and that republic is poor which is not governed by noble men selected by its citizens.

The signs of decay in the life of a nation show themselves as soon as anywhere else in the character of the men who are called to govern it. When they seek their own ends, and not the public weal; when they abandon principles, and administer according to the personal interest of cliques and parties; when they forsake righteousness, and call upon greedy, insatiable selfishness for counsel; and

[1] Died March 11, 1874. Sunday evening discourse in Plymouth Church.

when the laws and the whole framework of the government are but so many instruments of oppression and of wrong, then the nation cannot be far from decadence. When God means to do well by a nation that has back-slidden, among the earliest tokens of His benef-icent intent is the restoration of men of integ-rity and of honour—men who live for their fellows, and not for themselves.

I propose to look back a little to-night over that great period of decadence with which so many of us are too familiar, but which must not be forgotten, lest the lesson which it teaches should also perish.

The beginnings of our land, as you remem-ber, were eminently religious. Our fathers came hither to establish a new and notable dispensation, seeking to lay it upon founda-tions of righteousness. For generations they succeeded; and here was developed that con-summate form of liberty which carried out, as it could not be carried out in antiquity, the idea of the freedom of the whole people.

It was here that France lit her torch; but she knew not how to follow our example. To a large extent it was from this land that liberty derived in Europe its modern impetus. We ourselves derived the seed of liberty from

Holland and from England ; but we planted it here under a free sky and upon a noble soil ; and from this seed which we brought hither we reared a harvest; and we sent back and resowed in France, in Germany, and through-out Europe, it would seem now, the same blessed truths which have emancipated us.

But " when the sons of God came to present themselves before the Lord, Satan came also among them ; " and when our institutions were framed for liberty and for righteousness, there was permitted to be twined among them an element false in morals, corrupt in political economy, and utterly subversive of all rights and doctrines of human liberty. And there came to be developed also a procedure which, while it gave partial benefit to a favoured class, corrupted the whole system of industry, not alone in the immediate field where this pro-cedure was established—namely, in the slave-holding States of the Union—but indirectly, and by the circulation, as it were, in the whole body politic. For slavery is essential treason to free labour, and to the rights of the work-ing man, the world over. It is esteemed bad enough for labour to be indebted to capital ; but it was worse a thousand times when cap-ital owned not only labour but the labourer too ; and that was the condition over the fairest portion of this continent.

Organized into our affairs, the principle of slavery influenced national history in such a way as to inevitably produce interior antagonism, clash, and grating of interests. When the Mississippi and the Missouri come together, and their waters push each other every whither, and their face is covered with eddies and wrinkles, it is in vain for the Mississippi to reproach the Missouri; and it is in vain for the eastward-coming river to reproach the southward-coming river. It is not the fault of either of them that they scowl upon each other. There is a law that makes it unavoidable. So, that democracy which developed freedom in labour, and that aristocracy which developed bondage in labour, in the same government, could not keep their hands off from each other. They were born antagonists, and conflict between them was a necessity.

There was, then, this latent principle of antagonism which threatened our existence. In the conflict which ensued, and which increased as the elements of liberty and slavery ripened into full expression in national life, there was more and more a corrupting of the morals and the conscience of the whole nation.

# Charles Sumner

The entire South was corrupted by perversion; for what the fathers believed to be a permissible evil, to be done away in the course of time, their descendants, when it became profitable in the fields of both money and politics, turned and justified. Although in the early days the opponents of slavery were eminently the ablest men of the South, in the more recent days all the leading men of the South—her scholars, her poets, her publicists, and her ministers—all joined in one great outcry to justify slavery, and to make it the very foundation of national life, as well as the very philosophy of national thrift. So the whole South went wrong, under the influence of slavery; and it was taught in her schools and her colleges, until a whole generation had been brought up from the cradle in the doctrine of its essential beneficence, and of its wisdom in political economy. It is in vain to say that the people of the South did not believe this doctrine. The younger men of the South did believe it. It came to them almost with their growth. But none the less were they perverted and corrupted by it.

The North was yet more corrupted, because her interests led her largely to placate and defer to the South. Nothing can be more melancholy, particularly for the Eastern part of our land, than to remember the public sentiment which existed in churches, when it was made an offense that almost ostracized a man to plead in a prayer-meeting for slaves ; when men bated their breath in speaking of human rights ; when pulpits not only were dumb, but were employed very largely in the defense or palliation of slavery, or only admitted in an underbreath that it was an evil—an evil which must be borne with patiently. If there was not apology for slavery, there was at least a guilty silence concerning it during a long period in the pulpits of the North.

The benevolent associations of the North— especially those men who were relied upon to carry out the essential parts of their work— were wrapt up in complicity with this great mischief, and refused to bear their testimony. I will not go into detail ; but you will remember how pitiful was the position of the great missionary and publishing societies of the Christian community in the North. Following their lead, the commercial publishers took out of their publications of every kind those great truths which had been the meat of generations before ; and in their reading-books nothing was said of liberty that could be construed as condemning American slavery. In none of their books for the use of schools was there anything that could offend the South. So fashion, commerce, religion, and politics throughout the North were lowered in tone; and they did obeisance to slavery. In politics, if possible, it was worse than anywhere else, by reason of ambition and political aspiration. From the peculiar position of affairs, no man in the North who hoped for preferment dared to speak on the subject of liberty. Every young lawyer was warned not to give way to intemperate enthusiasm in favour of freedom, because it would certainly block up all hope of his advancement. No man could hope to go to the Legislature of the State, and certainly not to the national Legislature, if he dared to utter an honest sentiment of liberty. Men were marked; and if they desired ready advancement, not simply must they be silent in regard to the sacredness of freedom, but they must say some kind and conciliatory things for slavery. When they did this, they were "*sound.*"

Therefore, it came to pass that there was bred a generation of men of whom the fathers in the upper sphere were ashamed. There were men in the North who were corrupted by the bribes which were presented to them by slavery. There were political eunuchs, emasculated men, fearing, calculating, tergiversating. We never had a period of more profound national humiliation than that between 1830 and 1860.

I myself came into public life about the year 1837, and I was a witness of this condition of things; so that I speak from my own knowledge. The great struggle at that time, I remember full well, was for liberty of thought and of expression. I was tutored. I had friends in high places who took me aside, and whispered in my ear, saying, " Prudence; caution; you have opportunity; good society is open to you: do not blight your prospects. There is a chance for you in public life: do not by rash speaking spoil your opportunity of ascending. Wait; consider; let your thoughts ripen." Muzzling and suffocation were the order of the day. I remember distinctly when Birney's press was mobbed, in Cincinnati, and dragged through the streets, and thrown into the Ohio River. I remember perfectly the night when I was one of those who patrolled the streets, armed, to defend the houses of the poor coloured people in that city. I remember when no prayer-meeting or church-gathering allowed men to speak on the subject of liberty. I remember when in Presbytery and Synod it was considered a heresy to advocate freedom. I remember when it was regarded as next to treason in politics for a man to be an avowed advocate of national liberty.

The battle began in the North on the question of whether liberty of thought, liberty of speech, and liberty of printing, should be maintained; and we went through days when the birds of fate laid addled eggs—and we had all we wanted of them; days of darkness and humiliation and disgrace.

The condition of Washington from 1830 to 1860 was worse than the court of Pharaoh while he held the Israelites in bondage. I speak not of its want of thrift; I speak not of its slatternly condition; I speak not of its lack of enterprise, I speak not of the smothering there of every element of prosperity : I speak of the moral degradation that prevailed there, and of the rod of iron which was held over the heads of all the men who went thither. Aggressive politics was there the order of the day. Among the movements in this direction was the passage of that blessed infamy, the Fugitive Slave Law. I say *blessed*, because that, perhaps, marked the time when reaction really set in. It was the most cruel insult to the conscience of Northern men, and the most needless, that was ever offered by men given over by fate to fatuity. There was no necessity for it. It was a defiance thrown in the face of the North.

Then came the Kansas struggle. Then came the repeal of the Missouri Compromise. Then came preparations for the nationalization of slavery. Then came the scheme for allowing slaves to go *in transitu* through the Northern States. Changes in the Constitution were contemplated by which slavery should be as national as liberty.

Those were the elements to which we had come when the war surprised us. Dark times were upon us then. I remember them full well. I had drunk in the love of liberty with the breath of my life. I do not remember an hour, in my very boyhood, in which my soul was not on fire for the rights of men. I never wavered. I never bent. Although I had the same desire for kindness and consideration and sympathy which every generous and unperverted heart has, I never saw the moment when I would buy popularity or position in society by yielding one hair's-breadth of my feeling of enthusiastic conscience for human rights, and for rights that were sacred in proportion as they were denied to men, and in proportion as men were poor, and crude, and unhelpful of themselves.

I well remember groaning and travailing in spirit through all those dark days. I did not altogether give up hope; but, from the year 1856 to the year 1860, events trod so fast on each other that I confess to so much relinquishment of hope that I feared that perhaps God meant to break this Nation in pieces to teach the nations of the earth the guilt and delusion of human bondage. I could not bear it; and many a prayer in this Plymouth house, many a prayer in my own closet, many a prayer in the highway, and many a prayer in the forest, have I sent up, that our Nation might be spared and purged, rather than destroyed for the benefit of posterity.

The mercy of God was seen early, in raising up an army of men to resist the mischiefs that were threatened to the country. Private men there were not a few who enlisted in the cause of freedom. There was Garrison, the uncompromising and harsh truth-teller. There was the fiery Weld, like a second Peter the Hermit. There was the patrician Phillips, who never spoke without piercing—whose tongue was a rapier. There was May, of sweeter heart, and equally noble courage. There was Jackson, who, though not known, was one of those secret sources of supply and influence which determined events. There were the two Tappans, one of whom was long with us in this church. There was Joshua Leavitt, a citizen of Brooklyn until a year or two ago, when he departed. There was Rogers, who died of a broken heart early in the struggle. There were Whittier, and Longfellow, and Lowell, and Emerson, and others, of whom I shall speak again.

It is often said that the church of the North was corrupted. At one period, it certainly was guilty. Nor did we have the help of the great majority of the churches of the North in the Eastern States until a comparatively late period of the conflict. But I can say, to the credit of the New-school Presbyterian church of the West, with which my lot was cast, that, before the year 1837, it was effectually leavened by liberty. The first vote that I ever cast in the Presbyterian Church was a vote that the Presbytery of Indianapolis should never receive a licentiate, or should never license any man, who held slaves, unless he would show to us that he held them unwillingly, and that he would as soon as possible give them up. My impression is that there was not in the New-school Presbyterian Church in Indiana a minister who was not in favour of liberty. Long before the church in the East was aroused on the subject of slavery, the Western church stood established in opposition to it. The ministers of the New-school Presbyterian Church in the West were early and faithful labourers for emancipation.

Of public men we shall not soon forget the mission of John Quincy Adams. Many of you have forgotten the noble tasks imposed upon himself by Governor Slade. There was Gerrit Smith and there was Alvan Stewart. There was Joshua Giddings, who early espoused the Anti-slavery cause. There was John P. Hale, who served it in the Senate. There was Seward, both in New York and in the Senate. There was Greeley, foremost among journalists. Still later was Sumner; and Thaddeus Stevens; and later yet, Lincoln, and his great war-minister, Stanton. These, and many others whom time would fail me to mention, were the men who appeared, to turn back the captivity, and establish the glory and radiance of universal liberty.

Then came the blinding of the wise and the

weakening of the strong. Then came the fatuity of Southern leadership. Had the leaders of the South been wise, we might still have been enthralled. Time and again it seemed to me that, not being wise, if they had been at least cunning, they still would have held empire. But " whom the gods would destroy they first make mad."

There has recently been an extraordinary conjunction. Two men have departed from us in the same week. The funeral services of the one overlap those of the other. They were both representative men—he of Boston and he of Buffalo. Mr. Millard Fillmore, in private life, was an irreproachable man, amiable, kind, and universally to be respected ; but as a public man, he was a type of that weakness and cowardice which was bred in the North by the accursed influence of slavery in the South. Charles Sumner was the representative man of that reactionary spirit which was developed by liberty contending for its old rights and for its old ground. These two men have died almost at the same time ; and although I would not invade the sanctity of the grave, it befits historical reminiscence that these two antithetical men, one representing the old, and the other representing the new, within the period of a week going out from the generation of the living, should be mentioned in this contrast.

Personally, privately, I honour Mr. Fillmore; but as a public man he had no political conscience. He was without any apparent sympathy for any of those principles on which this great Nation was founded. He gave to a party —a miserable party—that which belonged to the higher interests of humanity and of mankind. He gave up Liberty to be crucified between Southern Slavery and Northern Mammon; and then washed his hands, and said, "I am innocent of the blood of this just person."

Of another sort was Charles Sumner. By his birth, by his education, by his social surroundings, he was fitted to be an aristocrat; nor was his disposition averse to such a place and title, for by nature he was self-considering. He was so intense in his own convictions as to become arrogant, and impose his views upon others with a species of oratorical despotism. But from the beginning of his life a romantic moral sense allied him to justice, to rectitude; and since in our day justice was most flagrantly violated by slavery, his love of justice and of truth took him, to his honour and to the glory of mankind, out from his class, and away from aristocracy, and made, essentially, an intellectual democrat of him. Personally he never was democratic. Intellectually he became so, by the force of the struggle of the day in which he lived.

I cannot but call to mind how strangely, and how very nobly, the old elect families of the commonwealth of the glorious old State of Massachusetts behaved. They were a genuine aristocracy, both of wealth and of historic association ; and yet, what more noble man of the people was there in Massachusetts than Adams ? Where have we found a man more nobly allied to liberty in the day of its peril than he was ? What higher credit rested upon any household than that which came from the name of Quincy ? Fathers and sons —how true they were ! *Aristocrats* do you call them ? They were the truest *democrats !*

Longfellow, naturally tender and refined, shrinking from struggle and from the rude rush of unwashed multitudes, did not disdain to set his harp, in the earliest hours, and sing songs of liberty, when it was to bring upon him discords and howlings, and not the music of praise. Emerson, the calm, the observational, the coolly reflecting, had not warmth enough to make him an enthusiast in religion ;

but he had patriotism and humanity to make him bear steadfast witness in the teeth of slavery. Whittier, the beautiful singer who wraps indignation and wrath about with such gentleness of spirit, Quaker-like—he could write "Ichabod" on the great name of Webster and doom him as though he had struck him with lightning, and yet all the time could seem as sweet as the Gospel. And there was the elegant patrician, the son of aristocratic sires, born sovereign, full of culture and of exquisite refinement, a noble man—Phillips, who put aside all ambitions, who devoted himself to the thankless task of speaking to mobs, and who, through good report and through evil report, carried his lance, and never once had it shivered or cast vilely away, and lived to see triumphant the cause which he loved.

In this band, of which I have not enumerated the half, belonged Charles Sumner; and by force of circumstances he became its leader, being advanced to eminent trusts. He came forth at the time when such men as Story, Webster, Choate, and Everett were the heroes of Massachusetts. I remember that it was as much as a man's life was worth then to speak in derogation of Daniel Webster; but how do men feel respecting him to-day? I remember when Choate was as brilliant as a star. Now he is as a meteor, the memory of which has gone with its radiance. And Everett—his last days were his best days; and all that he did in elegant literature was not so much as he did when he wrote in Mr. Bonner's *Ledger* for the people,—because, then, for the first time, I think, Edward Everett stood among common folks, in sympathy with them, and employed his culture, and reason, and taste, and genius, for the masses. In all the great and masterful struggles for liberty, and for the redemption of our land, neither Choate nor Webster nor Everett was found in the van.

Charles Sumner was endowed by nature with a noble presence. He was physically of a most manly type. He had an admirably constituted mind; and yet he was not a child of genius. His learning, joined to his high moral sense, constituted him what he was. He was a *made* man. He was well versed in law, in general literature, in history, in art, and in *belles lettres*. He was fitted in all these respects to carry to his sphere in the United States Senate great influence and great power. He carried there an industry which was almost unmatched, and a straightforwardness and unchanging intent which was well-nigh without a parallel. The meaning of his life, the force of all his enthusiasm, was, *Bondage must be destroyed, and Liberty must be established.* For that he became a martyr. He has died, lately, and from the blow in 1856 that felled him in the Senate chamber, that darkened many years of his life, and that gave to him a shock which his nervous system never recovered from. Not John Brown himself, nor Lincoln, was more a martyr for liberty than Charles Sumner has been. How glorious such a death as his! How well it beseems his reputation! Better so. Now, no pitying. As, when a man is knighted, the sovereign takes the sword and smites him on the shoulder, and says, " Rise up, Sir Charles ! " so the club that smote Sumner on the head did more than knight him—it brought him to honour and to immortality.

His devotion, his suffering, his perseverance, have been without faltering. He filled nobly the place where God put him. God worked largely by him in the restoration of conscience in the politics and statesmanship of this Nation, and to-day the whole country stands still to honour the name of Charles Sumner.

No son bears his name. No family will transmit it to the future. No descendant will gaze fondly upon his pictured face, and say, " It was my ancestor." He and his kindred are cut off. But the old State that gave him birth, and that he served so nobly, shall cut his name in letters so deep that time itself shall never rub them out; and no man shall ever read the history of these United States of America, and fail to see, shining brightly, with growing lustre through the ages, the name of Charles Sumner. No son, no daughter, weeps for him; but down a million dusky cheeks there are tears trickling. They whom he served weep for him. He was the Moses that helped to bring out of bondage myriads of the oppressed, who to-day feel that a father and a protector is gone up from among them ; and I would rather have the sympathy, the sorrow, and the prayers of the smitten than all the eulogies and all the honours of strong and prosperous men. He has lived well. He has died well. His faults will go down with him. His virtues will live after him. He joined himself to whatever was best in his time. Now he is with God.

Young men, let me speak a few words to you in respect to some parts of the example of this man who has departed from our midst.

First, you will take notice that he identified his own interests with the noblest interests of his country. He was not a vermin statesman, a parasitic statesman, who looked upon his country but as a carcass from which he might draw blood. In a venal, corrupt time, he held trust and power unsullied and unsuspected. Nothing can speak better for the judgment of corrupt men than the fact that they never dared to approach him—for Mr. Sumner said, with inimitable *naïveté*, " People speak of Washington as being corrupt. I do not believe a word of it; I have been in Washington fifteen years and more, and I have never seen a particle of corruption ! " No, he never had. He was the last man that any corrupt schemer dared to approach.

It is not necessary that men should be greedy, and selfish, and corrupt, in order to be prosperous. The foremost man of his time has died with white hands and a clean heart.

His patriotism sought no aggrandizement of his nation by defrauding others. His was not a belligerent nor a selfish statesmanship. He attempted to associate this land of his love

with the best interests of mankind universally.
He was an advocate of peace. He preached
and inspired the sense of justice among nations. Known well in America and in Europe,
and esteemed among statesmen and courts and
lawyers everywhere, his voice was against
violence, and for amity based upon justice.
His ambition was not for the " manifest destiny" of greediness; it was for the better
destiny of temperance, forbearance, patience,
and plenitude of power for the defense of
ourselves, but yet more for the defense of the
poor and of the needy. Everywhere aggres-
sion met his determined resistance. He was
a statesman because he based all procedure on
great principles. He was a republican statesman because he sought the welfare of all ; and
not of a privileged class. In his case this is
the more noticeable because his personal habits
did not lead him to love association with common people. It was principle, and not personal attraction, that moved him. In some
sense, it may be said that he denied himself,
and loved those who were beneath him. Nay,
I think he thought more of mankind than he
did of men. I think he loved the principles
of justice and of liberty, rather than liberty
and justice themselves. It was because liberty

in practical life glorified the principle of liberty that he loved it.

He is an example of personal integrity—an example not a little needed. Much assaulted, much misunderstood, partly from his own fault, and partly from circumstances, nevertheless he was prosperous, and had an illustrious career, never drooping, and never blackened by any taint. He has died in honour; and his name remains a glorious name in the galaxy of American patriots.

Sumner was a man of courage, of fidelity to convictions. He never meanly calculated. He never asked the question whether it was dangerous to speak. He was one of those heroic spirits that carried the fight further than it needed to be carried. He erred by an excess of bravery. He was a self-sacrificing man, giving up every prospect of life for the sake of doing his duty and establishing rectitude. He lost his life, and found it. He has verified the truth that disinterestedness is not inconsistent with the highest ambition. We have not a great many such men. There is not a disposition, in this vast, trading, thriving, commercial nation, and in this time of greed, to believe in romantic heroism of character; and it is good for us to be called to the consideration of a man who did not live for himself, and whose nature, revolving about itself, was trained by the principle of justice to develop itself for the welfare of others. I cannot conceive of a man who by nature befitted the courtly circle better than he. If I had looked through all the old State of Massachusetts, I could not have found, it seems to me, one man who would have been more likely to ally himself to government, to party and to illustrious power than Charles Sumner; and it was a marvel of the providence of God to see this man, who was built apparently to play the part of a sovereign and an aristocrat, filling the office of nurse to the slave child; giving his brilliant knowledge, his unwearied industry, and the fruit which he had gathered from every field, to those who needed succour; and bringing the stores of his literary attainments, the richness of his historical researches, and the accumulated treasures of the ages, which were his, and employing them to build better huts for the emancipated bondmen.

If he does not rank with the earlier men of our history; if he does not rank with the inventive geniuses of the age to which he belonged; yet no man in America has ever surpassed Charles Sumner in the entire dedication of the gifts which God granted him to the service of the poor and needy. Thousands and thousands are blessed by him who have only heard his name to rail at it; for while he secured rights to the poor, and while he removed disabilities from those who were enthralled, not only the particular class for whom he specially laboured were benefited, but every honest man in the country, whatever might be his nationality, participated in the bounty which he wrought out.

He has gone to his reward. He has lived a noble and spotless life on earth. He has not been a hero without a blemish; and yet his blemishes were not spots of taint. His faults were weaknesses, not crimes of the soul. They were intensities, partaking somewhat of fierceness, engendered by the high conflicts through which he passed. And let us forget them. Let us bury them, as we bury the noble form, dust to dust, under the sod. Let us remember his virtue, his integrity, his self-devotion, his enormous industry, his patient humanity, and his endurance unto the end as a martyr for liberty.

## VII

## WENDELL PHILLIPS[1]

IT was on last Wednesday that, standing upon the steps of the Parker House, Boston, in School Street, my attention was arrested by a procession. As they came up, I saw a soldierly body of coloured men with muskets reversed, the silent band following, with officers' corps behind it, their swords reversed, and then the carriages, following the hearse that bore—dust to dust—all that remained on earth of Wendell Phillips. The streets could not hold the crowd, and he whom the mob had sought once and again to tear to pieces now drew tears on every side from the mob, and the obsequious city sought to make up its vulgar scorn of other days by its worshipful attention.

It is respecting this man and his times that I shall, very briefly and imperfectly, speak this morning.

[1] Discourse in Plymouth Church, Sunday morning, February 10, 1884.

# Wendell Phillips

Fifty years ago, during my college life in Amherst, I was chosen by the Athenian Society to debate the question of African Colonization, which then was new, fresh and enthusiastic.  Garrison was then just kindling into that firebrand that never went out until slavery was consumed.  Wendell Phillips, a young lawyer, had just begun his career. Fortunately, I was assigned to the negative side of the question, and in preparing to speak I prepared my whole life.  I contended against colonization as a condition of emancipation,— enforced colonization was but little better than enforced slavery,—and advocated immediate emancipation on the broad ground of human rights.  I knew but very little then, but I knew this, that all men are designed of God to be free, a fact which ought to be the text of every man's life—this sacredness of humanity as given of God, redeemed from animalism by Jesus Christ, crowned and clothed with rights that no law nor oppression should dare touch.

Nearly two generations have passed since then ; the young men who are marching now from youth to manhood are little acquainted with the men or movements of those days, but a few gray heads are left that can recall all these scenes.  It has been said that men are more ignorant of that part of history which immediately precedes their own lives, than of any other. Let us, therefore, throw some little light upon the history of those days that immediately precede our own.

At the beginning, in the history of this people, Slavery was the accident : it was introduced at a time before the world's eyes had been opened ; it came in, indeed, under the cover of benevolence ; it had not attained a very great estate for many years ; and yet, in the days of its infancy, it so conflicted with the fundamental ideas on which our institutions and laws were based, that the Northern States got rid of it. Because the climate and husbandry were not favourable to it in the Northern States, they were helped to do it ; but the spirit of liberty had taken on the moral element in New England, in New York, and in Pennsylvania ; and slavery was soon extinguished. In the South it became a very important industrial element. Rice, sugar, cotton were the trinity that dominated the industry of the South, and slave labour was favourable to this simple industry. It became, therefore, a pecuniary interest to the South, as it never was in the North. After a time the industry became so important that, although throughout all the South in the earlier days, men recognized slavery as a sin, and its existence as a great misfortune, and always hoped that the day would speedily come for emancipation; yet all those hopes and expectations were met and resisted and overthrown by the fact that slavery became a political interest. It became the centre which united every Southern State with every other, and gave unity to the party of the South; so that political reasons, rooted in pecuniary reasons, gave great strength to slavery and its propagandism in the South. The North emancipated; the South fortified.

It has been said a thousand times, and every time falsely (it was said by one of the most eloquent sons of the South a few months ago in Cooper Union, where I presided, but it was not the time nor a fitting place to expose the misstatement), it has been said that the North sold out, and having realized on their slaves invested in liberty as a better paying stock.

This statement is absolutely untrue. It has no historical verity in Massachusetts. There, to some slight extent, slavery existed as it did not in Vermont, New Hampshire, and Maine, but died by a very simple legal decision, one case having been brought into the courts, and the courts determining that it was inconsistent with the Declaration of Independence, and the Constitution sequent; and the man stood free. After that there was no enactment; nothing. Slavery perished of itself by that one single decision.

In New York a bill was passed early for the gradual emancipation of slaves, and it was guarded in every way. On attaining a certain age slaves were to become free; up to that age they were the property of their masters, upon whom the responsibility of their support still rested with full weight. After a trial of some years it was considered a great deal better to be rid of the evil at once, and subsequent legislation determined immediate emancipation. Now, as against those that falsely accused the integrity and love of liberty of this great State, let me say that if you will go back to the laws, and to the practice under them, you shall find that with the declaration of emancipation, both the primitive form of it and the subsequent form of it, the right of the slave or of the coming freedman was guaranteed, and his safety.

No man was permitted to take a slave out of the State of New York without giving bond for his return, and if he came back without his slave, unless he could prove that the slave had died, he was himself made a criminal, and subjected to criminal punishment; and there is reason to believe, in regard to the most of the comparatively few slaves that were in the State of New York, that their emancipation was a *bona fide* emancipation, and they never were sold South.

Now and then a man can steal a horse; but we should not lay to the State from which it was taken the charge of abetting theft. There may have been single men or women spirited away; there may have been thieving; I know of none, I have heard of none, though there may have been; but whatever the statute could do to maintain the slave in his integrity and liberty was done, and substantially and generally it was effectual; and all this cheap wash of wild declamation that we hear going through the land, to the effect that the North sold out its slaves and then went into the business of emancipation, is simply false.

The condition of the public mind throughout the North at the time that I came to the consciousness of public affairs, and was studying my profession, may be described as *the condition of imprisoned moral sense.* All men, almost, agreed together in saying that " Slavery is wrong; but what can we do?" The compromise of our fathers included us; and fidelity to the agreements that had been made in the formation of our Constitution, of our Confederation first, and of our Constitution afterwards, was regarded everywhere as a moral obligation by men that hated slavery. "The compromises of the Constitution must be respected," said the priest in the pulpit, said the politician in the field, said the statesman in public hall; and men abroad, in England especially, could not understand what was the reason of the later hesitancy of President Lincoln, and of the people, when they had risen to arms, in declaring at once the emancipation of the slaves. There never has been in history an instance more notable in which, I think, the feelings and the moral sense of so large a number of people have been held in check for reasons of fidelity to obligations assumed in their behalf; and I am bound to say that with all its faults and weaknesses there has never been an instance more noble. That being the underlying moral element, the commercial question in the North very soon became, on the subject of slavery, what the industrial and political questions of the South had made it. It corrupted the manufacturer and the merchant. Throughout the whole North every man that could make anything by it regarded the South as his legal, lawful market; for the South did not manufacture. They had the cheap and vulgar husbandry of slavery. They could make more money with cotton than with corn or beef, or pork, or leather, or hats, or woodenware. Our Northern ships went South to get their forest timbers, and brought them to Connecticut to be made into woodenware, and axe helves, and rake handles, and carried them right back to sell to the men whose axes had cut down the trees.

The South manufactured nothing except slaves; it was a great manufacture, that; and the whole market of the North was bribed. The harness-makers, the wagon-makers, the clock-makers, makers of all manner of implements and goods, were subject to this bribery. Every manufactory, every loom as it clanked in the North, said: " Maintain not slavery, but the compromises of the Constitution," for that was the veil under which all these cries were continually uttered.

The distinction between the Anti-slavery men and Abolitionists was simply this: the Abolitionist disclaimed the obligation to maintain this Government and the promise of the Constitution; the Anti-slavery man recognized the binding obligation of the Constitution, and sought the emancipation of slaves by a more circuitous and gradual influence: but Abolitionism covered both terms. It was regarded, however, throughout the North as a greater sin than Slavery itself; and none of you that are under thirty years of age can form an adequate conception of the public sentiment and feeling during the days of my young manhood. A man that was known to be an Abolitionist had better be known to have the plague. Every door was shut to him. If he was born under circumstances that admitted him to the best society, he was the black sheep of the family. If he aspired, by fidelity, industry and genius, to good society, he was debarred. "An Abolitionist" was enough to put the mark of Cain upon any young man that arose in my early day, and until I was forty years of age, it was punishable to preach on the subject of liberty. It was enough to expel a man from church communion if he insisted on praying in the prayer-meeting for the liberation of the slaves. I am speaking the words of truth and soberness. The Church was dumb in the North, but not in the West.  A marked distinction exists be-tween the history of the new school of Pres-byterian churches in the West and the Con-gregational churches, the Episcopal churches, the Methodist and Baptist churches in the North and East.  The great publishing so-cieties that were sustained by the contributions of the churches were absolutely dumb.  Great controversies raged round about the doors of the Bible Society, of the Tract Society and of the American Board of Commissioners for Foreign Missions.  The managers of these societies resorted to every shift except that of sending the Gospel to the slaves.  They would not send the Bible to the South ; for, they said, " It is a punishable offense in most of the Southern States to teach a slave to read ; and are we to go in the face of this State legislation and send the Bible South ? "  The Tract Society said : " We are set up to preach the Gospel, not to meddle with political and industrial institutions."  And so they went on printing tracts against tobacco and its uses, tracts against dancing and its abuses, and re-fusing to print a tract that had a shadow of criticism on slavery !

One of the most disgraceful things took place in New Jersey.  I have the book.  It was an edition of the Episcopal prayer-book. They had put into the front of it a steel engraving of Ary Scheffer's "Christus Consolator,"—Christ the Consoler. There was a semicircle around about the beneficent and aerial figure of our Saviour,—the poor, the old, the sick, the mother with her dead babe, bowed in grief; every known form of human sorrow belonged to the original design and picture; and among others a fettered slave, with his hands lifted to heaven praying for liberty: but this was too much; and so they cut out the slave, and left the rest of the picture, and bound it into the Episcopal prayer-book of New Jersey. I have a copy of it, which I mean to leave to the Historical Society of Brooklyn when I am done using it.

These things are important as showing the incredible condition of public sentiment at that time. If a man came known to be an Anti-slavery man it almost preluded bankruptcy in business.

You remember, some of you, the black list that was framed and sent all over the South, of men that were suspected of being Abolitionists in New York City. The South undertook to boycott the whole North. Then it was that I drew up the sentence for a then member of this church, " I have goods for sale, but not principles." Resistance was a blight to all political hope. No man could have the slightest expectation of rising in politics that did not bow the knee to Baal. A derisive laugh was the only answer with which exhortations to nobility and manhood were received. This public sentiment was worse in the North than it was anywhere else, and in the Northeast worse than in the West, on account of the extent of manufacturing and commerce here.

When I came to Brooklyn I was exhorted not to meddle with so unpopular a subject. " What is the use ? " was said to me by a venerable master in Israel ; " why should you lose your influence ? Why don't you go on and preach the Gospel ? " to which I replied, " I don't know any gospel of that kind. My gospel has in it the breaking of prison bars and shackles, the bringing forth of prisoners, and if I can't preach that I won't preach at all." The very first sermon that I ever preached before this congregation—or rather, the congregation that met me—was the declaration of my principles on temperance, on peace and war, and above all, on the subject of slavery. For years and years just prior to the renting of the pews, I came out like thunder on the subject of slavery; for I told my people that they need not think that they could dine me out of my principles, nor smooth me out of them, nor in any way make the pews an argument to me of prudence in the matter of principle.

The church rose steadily, despite the anti-slaveryism of the pastor. Yet, if a coloured man at that time had come into the church he would have been an object of observation, and the cause of some grumbling, though not of revolt in this church, thank God. There never has been a day since I became the pastor of Plymouth Church that a cleanly-dressed respectable coloured man or woman could not have come in and taken a seat here. It would have excited among a great many a good deal of trouble; but this congregation has been of that mind, and never the result of my undertaking to enforce it. I never preached on that subject. I never said to the people in this congregation, from the beginning to this day, " You ought to let coloured folks sit in your pew." I preached the dignity of man as a child of God; and lifted up the sanctity of human life and nature before the people. They made the application, and they made it wisely and well.

# Wendell Phillips

When I came here there was no place for coloured men and women in the theatre except the negro pen; no place in the opera; no place in the church except the negro pew; no place in any lecture hall; no place in the first-class car on the railways. The white omnibus of Fulton Ferry would not allow coloured persons to ride in it. They were never allowed to sit even in the men's cabin on the boats.

I invited Fred. Douglass, one day, in those times, to come to church here. "I should be glad to, sir," said he; "but it would be so offensive to your congregation." "Mr. Douglass, will you come? and if any man objects to it, come up and sit on my platform by me. You will always be welcome there."

I mention these things simply to show what was the state of feeling that existed everywhere twenty-five or thirty years ago. Existed! Swept through the land as a sultry sirocco sweeps through the desert, scorching and blasting public sentiment!

It was at the beginning of this Egyptian era in America that the young aristocrat of Boston appeared. His blood came through the best colonial families. He was an aristocrat by descent and by nature—a noble one, but a thorough aristocrat. All his life and power assumed that guise. He was noble, he was full of kindness to inferiors, he was willing to be and do and suffer for them; but he was never of them, nor did he ever equal himself to them. He was always above them; and his gifts of love were always the gifts of a prince to his subjects. All his life long he resented every attack on his person and on his honour as a noble aristocrat would. When they poured the filth of their imaginations upon him, he cared no more for it than the eagle cares what the fly is thinking about him away down under the cloud. All the miserable traffickers, all the scribblers and all the aristocratic boobies of Boston were no more to him than mosquitoes are to the behemoth or to the lion. He was aristocratic in his pride, and lived higher than most men lived. He was called of God as truly as ever Moses and the Prophets were: not exactly for the same great ends, but in consonance with those great ends.

The elder ones remember when Lovejoy was infamously slaughtered by a mob in Alton, and blood was shed that has been the seed of liberty all over this land. I remember it. At this time, it was, that Channing lifted up his voice, and declared that the moral sentiment of Boston ought to be uttered in rebuke of that infamy and cruelty, and asked for Faneuil Hall in which to call a public meeting. This was indignantly refused by the Common Council of Boston. Being a man of wide influence, he gathered around about himself enough venerable and influential old citizens of that city to make a denial of their united request a perilous thing ; and Faneuil Hall was granted to call a public meeting to express itself on this subject of the murder of Lovejoy. The meeting was made up largely of rowdies. They meant to overawe and put down all other expressions of opinion except those that then rioted with the riotous. United States District Attorney Austin (when Wendell Phillips' name is written in letters of light on one side of the monument, down low on the other side, and spattered with dirt, let the name of Austin also be written) made a truculent speech, and justified the mob, and ran the whole career of the sewer of those days, and justified non-interference with slavery. Wendell Phillips, just come to town as a young lawyer without at present any practice, almost unknown except to his own family, fired with the infamy, and feeling called of God in his soul, went upon the platform. His first utterances brought down the hisses of the mob. He was not a man very easily subdued by any mob. They listened as he kindled and poured on that man Austin the fire and lava of a volcano ; and he finally turned the course of the feeling of the meeting. Practically unknown when the sun went down one day, when it rose the next morning all Boston was saying, " Who is this fellow ? who is this Phillips ? "—a question that has never been asked since !

Thenceforth he was a flaming advocate of liberty, with singular advantages over all other pleaders. Mr. Garrison was not noted as a speaker ; his tongue was his pen. Mr. Phillips was not much given to the pen, his pen was his tongue, and no other like speaker has ever graced our history. I do not undertake to say that he surpassed all others. He had an intense individuality, and that intense individuality ranked him among the noblest orators that have ever been born to this continent, or I may say to our mother land. He adopted in full the tenets of Garrison, which were excessively disagreeable to the whole public mind. The ground which he took was that which Garrison took. Seeing that the conscience of the North was smothered and mute by reason of supposed obligations to the compromises of the Constitution, Garrison declared that the compromises of the Constitution were covenants with hell, and that no man was bound to observe them. This extreme ground Mr. Phillips also took—immediate, unconditional, universal emancipation at any cost whatsoever. That was Garrisonism; that was Wendell Phillipsism; and it would seem as though the Lord rather leaned that way too.

I shall not discuss the merits of Mr. Garrison nor of Mr. Phillips in every direction. I shall say that while the duty of immediate emancipation without conditions was unquestionably the right ground, yet in the providence of God even that could not be brought to pass except through the mediation of very many events. It is a remarkable thing that Mr. Phillips and Mr. Garrison both renounced the Union and denounced the Union in the hope of destroying slavery; whereas the providence of God protected the love of the Union when it was assailed by the South, and made the love of the Union the enthusiasm that carried through the great war of Emancipation. It was the very antithesis of the ground which they took. Like John Brown, Mr. Garrison;

like John Brown, Mr. Phillips; of a heroic spirit, seeking the great end nobly, but by measures not well adapted to directly secure the end.

Little by little the controversy spread. I shall not trace it. I am giving you simply the atmosphere in which Mr. Phillips sprang into being and into power. His career was a career of thirty or forty years of undiminished eagerness. He never quailed nor flinched, nor did he ever at any time go back one step, or turn in the slightest degree to the right or left. He gloried in his cause, and in that particular aspect of it which had selected him.

He stood on this platform. It is a part of the sweet and pleasant memories of my comparative youth here, that when the mob refused to let him speak in the Broadway Tabernacle before it was moved up-town—the old Tabernacle—William A. Hall, now dead, a fervent friend and Abolitionist, had secured the Graham Institute, on Washington Street, in Brooklyn, wherein to hold a meeting where Mr. Phillips should be heard. I had agreed to pray at the opening of the meeting. On the morning of the day on which it was to have taken place, I was visited by the committee of that Institute (excellent gentlemen,

whose feelings will not be hurt, because they
are all now ashamed of it ; they are in heaven),
who said that in consequence of the great peril
that attended a meeting at the Institute, they
had withdrawn the liberty to use it, and paid
back the money, and that they called simply
to say that it was out of no disrespect to me,
but from fidelity to their supposed trust.
Well, it was a bitter thing. If there is anything on earth that I am sensitive to, it is the
withdrawing of the liberty of speech and
thought. Henry C. Bowen, who certainly has
done some good things in his lifetime, said to
me, " You can have Plymouth Church if you
want it." " How ? " " It is the rule of the
church trustees that the church may be let by
a majority vote when we are convened ; but if
we are not convened, then every trustee must
give his assent in writing. If you choose to
make it a personal matter, and go to every trustee, you can have it." He meanwhile undertook, with Mr. Hall, to put new placards over
the old ones, notifying men, quietly, that the
meeting was to be held here, and distributed
thousands and tens of thousands of handbills
at the ferries. No task was ever more welcome. I went to the trustees man by man.
The majority of them very cheerfully accorded

the permission. One or two of them were
disposed to decline and withhold it. I made
it a matter of personal friendship. " You and
I will break if you don't give me this permission ; " and they signed. So the meeting
glided from the Graham Institute to this house.
A great audience assembled. We had detect-
ives in disguise, and every arrangement made
to handle the subject in a practical form if the
crowd should undertake to molest us. The
Rev. Dr. R. S. Storrs consented to come and
pray ; for Mr. Wendell Phillips was by mar-
riage a near and intimate friend and relation
of his. The reporters were here—when were
they ever not ? A gentleman was called to
preside over the meeting who had been known
to be an Abolitionist almost from his cradle ;
but he was personally a timid man, though
morally courageous. When I put the sense of
the meeting that he should preside, he got up
and was so scared that he could not be heard.
He muttered that he thought some other man
might have been chosen. I called him by
name and said, " You are selected to preside,
sir." He got up again—" Will you be kind
enough to come up here and preside, sir ? "
And for fear that he would be worse bom-
barded by not doing it than he would by doing

it, he came up. Prayer was uttered. An explanatory statement was made. Mr. Phillips began his lecture; and you may depend upon it by this time the lion was in him, and he went careering on. His views were extreme, he made them extravagant. I remember at one point,—for he was a man without bluster; serene, self-poised, never disturbed in the least, —he made an affirmation that was very bitter, and a cry arose over the whole congregation. He stood still, with a cold, bitter smile on his face and look in his eye, and waited till they subsided, when he repeated it with more emphasis. Again the roar went through. He waited, and repeated it if possible more intensely; and he beat them down with that one sentence, until they were still and let him go on.

The power to discern right amid all the wrappings of interest and all the seductions of ambition was singularly his. To choose the lowly for their sake; to abandon all favour, all power, all comfort, all ambition, all greatness—that was his genius and glory. He confronted the spirit of the Nation and of the age. I had almost said, he set himself against nature, as if he had been a decree of God overriding all these other insuperable obstacles.

That was his function. Mr. Phillips was not
called to be a universal orator any more than
he was a universal thinker. In literature and
in history he was widely read; in person most
elegant; in manners most accomplished;
gentle as a babe; sweet as a new-blown rose;
in voice, clear and silvery. He was not a man
of tempests; he was not an orchestra of a
hundred instruments; he was not an organ,
mighty and complex. The Nation slept, and
God wanted a trumpet, sharp, far-sounding,
narrow and intense; and that was Mr. Phillips.
The long roll is not particularly agreeable in
music or in times of peace, but it is better
than flutes or harps when men are in a great
battle, or are on the point of it. His eloquence was penetrating and alarming. He
did not flow as a mighty Gulf Stream; he did
not dash upon the continent as the ocean does;
he was not a mighty rushing river. His eloquence was a flight of arrows; sentence after
sentence, polished, and most of them burning.
He shot them one after the other, and where
they struck they slew; always elegant, always
awful. I think scorn in him was as fine as I
ever knew it in any human being. He had
that sublime sanctuary in his pride that made
him almost insensitive to what would by other

men be considered obloquy. It was as if he said every day, in himself, " I am not what they are firing at. I am not there, and I am not that. It is not against me. I am infinitely superior to what they think me to be. They do not know me." It was quiet and unpretentious, but it was there. Conscience and pride were the two concurrent elements of his nature.

He lived to see the slave emancipated, but not by moral means. He lived to see the sword cut the fetter. After this had taken place he was too young to retire, though too old to gather laurels of literature or to seek professional honours. The impulse of humanity was not at all abated. His soul still flowed on for the great under-masses of mankind, though like the Nile it split up into diverse mouths, and not all of them were navigable.

After a long and stormy life his sun went down in glory. All the English-speaking people on the globe have written among the names that shall never die, the name of that scoffed, detested, mob-beaten Wendell Phillips. Boston, that persecuted and would have slain him, is now exceedingly busy in building his tomb and rearing his statue. The men that would not defile their lips with his name are to-day thanking God that he lived.

He has taught a lesson that the young will do well to take heed to—the lesson that the most splendid gifts and opportunities and ambitions may be best used for the dumb and the lowly. His whole life is a rebuke to the idea that we are to climb to greatness by climbing up on the backs of great men ; that we are to gain strength by running with the currents of life ; that we can from without add anything to the great within that constitutes man. He poured out the precious ointment of his soul upon the feet of that diffusive Jesus who suffers here in His poor and despised ones. He has taught the young ambitions too—that the way to glory is the way, oftentimes, of adhesion simply to principle ; and that popularity and unpopularity are not things to be known or considered. Do right and rejoice. If to do right will bring you into trouble, rejoice that you are counted worthy to suffer with God and the providences of God in this world.

He belongs to the race of giants, not simply because he was in and of himself a great soul, but because he bathed in the providence of God, and came forth scarcely less than a god ;

because he gave himself to the work of God upon earth, and inherited thereby, or had reflected upon him, some of the majesty of his master. When pigmies are all dead, the noble countenance of Wendell Phillips will still look forth, radiant as a rising sun—a sun that will never set. He has become to us a lesson, his death an example, his whole history an encouragement to manhood—to heroic manhood.

# VIII

## EULOGY ON GRANT[1]

ANOTHER name is added to the roll of
those whom the world will not willingly
let die. A few years since storm-clouds filled
his heaven, and obloquy, slander and bitter
lies rained down upon him.

The clouds are all blown away, under a
serene sky he laid down his life, and the Nation wept. The path to his tomb is worn
by the feet of innumerable pilgrims. The
mildewed lips of Slander are silent, and even
Criticism hesitates lest some incautious word
should mar the history of the modest, gentle,
magnanimous Warrior.

The whole Nation watched his passage
through humiliating misfortunes with unfeigned sympathy; the whole world sighed
when his life ended! At his burial the un-
sworded hands of those whom he had fought
lifted his bier and bore him to his tomb with
love and reverence.

[1] Delivered at Tremont Temple, Boston, October 22, 1885.
Grant's death occurred on July 18, 1885.

234

# Eulogy on Grant

Grant made no claim to saintship. He was a man of like passions, and with as marked limitations as other men. Nothing could be more distasteful to his honest, modest soul while living, and nothing more unbecoming to his memory, than lying exaggerations and fulsome flatteries.

Men without faults are apt to be men without force. A round diamond has no brilliancy. Lights and shadows, hills and valleys, give beauty to the landscape. The faults of great and generous natures are often overripe goodness, or the shadows which their virtues cast.

Three elements enter into the career of a great citizen:

That which his ancestry gives;
That which opportunity gives;
That which his will develops.

Grant came from a sturdy New England stock; New England derived it from Scotland; Scotland bred it, at a time when Covenanters and Puritans were made—men of iron consciences hammered out upon the anvil of adversity. From New England the stream flowed to the Ohio, where it enriched the soil till it brought forth abundant harvests of great men. When it was Grant's time to be born, he came forth without celestial portents, and his youth had in it no prophecy of his manhood. His boyhood was wholesome, robust, with a vigorous frame. With a heart susceptible of tender love, he yet was not social. He was patient and persistent. He loved horses, and could master them. That is a good sign.

Grant had no art of creating circumstances; opportunity must seek him, or else he would plod through life without disclosing the gifts which God hid in him. The gold in the hills cannot disclose itself. It must be sought and dug.

A sharp and wiry politician, for some reason of Providence, performed a generous deed, in sending young Grant to West Point. He finished his course there, distinguished as a skillful and bold rider, with an inclination to mathematics, with little taste for the theory and literature of war, but with sympathy for its external and material developments. In boyhood and youth he was marked by simplicity, candour, veracity and silence.

After leaving the Academy he saw service in Mexico, and afterwards in California, but without conspicuous results.

Then came a clouded period, a sad life of irresolute vibration between self-indulgence and aspiration, through intemperance. He resigned from the army, and at that time one would have feared that his life would end in eclipse. Hercules crushed two serpents sent to destroy him in his cradle. It was later in his life that Grant destroyed the enemy that " biteth like a serpent and stingeth like an adder."

At length he struck at the root of the matter. Others agree not to drink, which is good ; Grant overcame the *wish* to drink—which is better. But the cloud hung over his reputation for many years, and threatened his ascendency when better days came. Of all his victories, many and great, this was the greatest, that he conquered himself. His will was stronger than his passions.

Poor, much shattered, he essayed farming. Carrying wood for sale to St. Louis did not seem to be that for which he was created ; neither did planting crops, nor raising cattle.

Tanning is an honourable calling, and, to many, a road to wealth. Grant found no gold in the tan vat.

Then he became a listless merchant—a silent, unsocial and rather moody waiter upon petty traffic.

He was a good subaltern, a poor farmer, a

worse tanner, a worthless trafficker. Without civil experience, without literary gifts, too diffident to be ambitious, too modest to put himself forward, too honest to be a politician, he was of all men the least likely to attain eminence, and absolutely unfitted, apparently, for preëminence; yet God's providence selected him.

When the prophet Samuel went forth to anoint a successor to the impetuous and imperious King Saul, he caused all the children of Jesse to pass before him. He rejected one by one the whole band. At length the youngest called from among the flock came in, and the Lord said to Samuel, "Arise, this is *he*," and Samuel took the horn of oil and anointed him in the midst of his brethren, and the spirit of the Lord came upon him from that day forward.

Ordained was **Grant** with the ointment of war—black and sulphurous.

Had Grant died at the tan-yard, or from behind the counter, the world would never have suspected that it had lost a hero. He would have fallen as an undistinguishable leaf among the millions cast down every year. His time had not come. It was plain that he **had** no capacity to create his opportunity. It must find him out, or he would die ignoble and unknown!

It was coming! Already the clouds afar off were gathering. He saw them not. No figures were seen upon the dim horizon of the already near future.

The insulted flag; the garments rolled in blood; a million men in arms; the sulphurous smoke of battle; gory heaps upon desperate battle-fields; an army of slowly moving crippled heroes; graveyards populous as cities; they were all in the clouded horizon, though he saw them not!

Let us look upon the scene on which he was soon to exert a mighty energy.

This continent lay waiting through ages for the seed of civilization. At length a sower came forth to sow. While he sowed the good seed of liberty and Christian civilization, an enemy, darkling, sowed tares. They sprang up and grew together. The Constitution cradled both Slavery and Liberty. While yet ungrown they dwelt together in peace. They snarled in youth, quarrelled when half grown, and fought when of full age. The final catastrophe was inevitable. No finesse, no device or compromise could withstand the inevitable. The conflict began in Congress; it drifted into commerce ; it rose into the very air, and public sentiment grew hot, and raged in the pulpit, the forum, and in politics.

The South, like a queenly beauty, grew imperious and exacting ; the North, like an obsequious suitor, knelt at her feet, only to receive contempt and mockery.

Both parties, Whig and Democrat, drank of the cup of her sorcery. It killed the Whig party. The Democrat was tougher, and was only besotted. A few, like John the Baptist, were preaching repentance, but, like him, they were in the wilderness, and seemed rude and shaggy fanatics.

If a wise moderation had possessed the South, if they had conciliated the North, if they had met the just scruples of honest men, who, hating slavery, dreaded the dishonour of breaking the compacts of the Constitution, the South might have held control for another hundred years. It was not to be. God sent a strong delusion upon them.

Nothing can be plainer than that all parties in the State were drifting in the dark, without any comprehension of the elemental causes at work. Without prescience or sagacity, like ignorant physicians, they prescribed at random; they sewed on patches, new compromise upon old garments ; they sought to conceal the real depth and danger of the gathering torrent by crying " Peace, peace ! " to each other. In short, they were seeking to medicate volcanoes and stop earthquakes by administering political quinine. The wise statesmen were bewildered and politicians were juggling fools.

The South had laid the foundation of her industry, her commerce, and her commonwealth upon slavery. It was slavery that inspired her councils, that engorged her philanthropy, that corrupted her political economy and theology, that disturbed all the ways of active politics ; broke up sympathy between North and South. As Ahab met Elijah with, " Art thou he that troubleth Israel ? " so Slavery charged the sentiments of Freedom with vexatious meddling and unwarrantable interference.

The South had builded herself upon the rock of Slavery. It lay in the very channels of civilization, like some Flood Rock lying sullen off Hell Gate. The tides of controversy rushed upon it and split into eddies and swirling pools, bringing incessant disaster. The rock would not move. It must be removed. It was the South itself that furnished the engineers. Arrogance in council sank the shaft, Violence chambered the subterranean passages, and Infatuation loaded them with infernal dynamite. All was secure. Their rock was their fortress. The hand that fired upon Sumter exploded the mine, and tore the fortress to atoms. For one moment it rose into the air like spectral hills —for one moment the waters rocked with wild confusion, then settled back to quiet, and the way of civilization was opened!

The spark that was kindled at Fort Sumter fell upon the North, like fire upon autumnal prairies. Men came together in the presence of this universal calamity with sudden fusion. They forgot all separations of politics, parties, or even of religion itself. It was a conflagration of patriotism. The bugle and the drum rang out in every neighbourhood, the plough stood still in the furrow, the hammer dropped from the anvil, book and pen were forgotten, pulpit and forum, court and shop, felt the electric shock. Parties dissolved and reformed. The Democratic party sent forth a host of noble men, and swelled the Republican ranks, and gave many noble leaders and irresistible energy to the Hosts of War. The whole land became a military school.

When once the North had organized its armies, there was soon disclosed an amiable folly of conciliation. It hoped for some peaceable way out of the war; generals seemed to fight so that no one should be hurt; they saw the mirage of future parties above the battle-field, and anxiously considered the political effect of their military conduct. They were fighting not to break down rebellion, but to secure a future presidency—or governorship. The South had smelted into a glowing mass. It believed in its course with an infatuation that would have been glorious if the cause had been better! It put its whole soul into war—and struck hard!

The South fought throughout for slavery and independence. The North fought for Union, but at first its leaders seemed aiming chiefly at securing political success after the War. Thus for two years, not unmarked by great deeds, the war lingered. Lincoln, sad and sorrowful, felt the moderation of his generals, and longed for a man of iron mould, who had but two words in his military vocabulary, VICTORY or ANNIHILATION.

He was coming! He was heard from at Forts Henry and Donelson.

Four great names were rising to sight—Sherman, Thomas, Sheridan; and larger than either, Grant! With his advent the armies, with some repulses, went steadily forward, from conquering to conquer. Aside from all military qualities, he had one absorbing spirit —the Union must be saved, the rebellion must be beaten, the Confederate armies must be threshed to chaff as on a summer threshing floor. He had no political ambition, no imaginary reputation to preserve or gain. A great genius for grand strategy, a comprehension of complex and vast armies, caution, prudence and silence while preparing, an endless patience, an indomitable will, and a real, downright fighting quality.

Thus at length Grant was really born! He had lain in the nest for long as an infertile egg. The brooding of War hatched the egg, and an eagle came forth!

It is impossible to reach the full measure of Grant's military genius until we survey the greatness of this most extraordinary war of modern days, or it may be said of any age.

For more than four years there were more than a million men on each side, stretched out upon a line of between one and two thousand miles, and a blockade rigorously enforced along a coast of an equal extent. During that time, counting no battle in which there were not five hundred Union men engaged, there were fought more than two thousand engagements—two thousand two hundred and sixty-one of record.

Amid this sea of blood, there shot up great battles, that for numbers, fighting and losses, will rank with the great battles of the world.

In 1862 the losses by death, wounds and missing on both sides, as extracted from Government Records, were nearly half a million.

Over 26,000 Northern soldiers died in captivity. If we reckon all who perished in field and hospital on both sides, nearly a million died in that War.

The number must be largely swelled if we add all who died at home, of sickness and wounds received in the campaigns.

The Secretary of War, in his report, dated November 22, 1865, makes the following remarks, which show more than anything else the spirit animating the people of the loyal States: "On several occasions, when troops were promptly needed to avert impending disaster, vigorous exertion brought them into the field from remote States with incredible speed. Official reports show that after the disasters on the Peninsula, in 1862, over 80,000 troops were enlisted, organized, armed, equipped, and sent into the field in less than a month. Sixty thousand troops have repeatedly gone to the field within four weeks. Ninety thousand infantry were sent to the armies from the five States of Ohio, Indiana, Illinois, Iowa, and Wisconsin, within twenty days. When Lee surrendered, thousands of recruits were pouring in, and men were discharged from recruiting stations and rendezvous in every State."

Into this sulphurous storm of war Grant entered almost unknown. It was with difficulty that he could obtain a command. Once set forward, *Donaldson*, *Shiloh*, *Vicksburg*, *Chickamauga*, *The Wilderness*, *Spottsylvania*, *Petersburg*, *Appomattox*, these were his footsteps. In four years he had risen, without political favour, from the bottom to the very highest command—not second to any living commander in all the world!

His plans were large, his undiscouraged will was patient to obduracy. He was not fighting for reputation, nor for the display of generalship, nor for a future Presidency. He had but one motive, and that as intense as life itself—the subjugation of the rebellion and the restoration of the broken Union. He embodied the feelings of the common people. He was their perfect representative. The war was waged for the maintenance of the Union, the suppression of armed resistance, and, at length, for the eradication of Slavery. Every step, from Donelson to Appomattox, evinced with increasing intensity this his one terrible purpose. He never wavered, turned aside, or dallied.

In all this career he never lost courage or equanimity. With a million men, for whose movements he was responsible, he yet carried a tranquil mind, neither depressed by disasters, nor elated by success. Gentle of heart, familiar with all, never boasting, always modest—Grant came of the old self-contained stock, men of a simple force of being, which allied his genius to the great elemental forces of Nature, silent, invisible, irresistible. When his work was done, and the defeat of Confederate armies was final, this dreadful man of blood was as tender towards his late adversaries as a woman towards her son. He imposed no humiliating conditions, spared the feelings of his antagonists, sent home the disbanded Southern men with food and with horses for working their crops, and when a revengeful spirit in the Executive Chair showed itself, and threatened the chief Southern generals, Grant indignantly interposed himself, and compelled his superior to relinquish his rash purpose.

There have been men—there are yet—for stupidity is long-lived—who regard Grant as only " a man of luck." Surely he was! Is it not luck through such an ancestry to have had conferred upon him such a body, such a disposition, such greatness of soul, such patriotism unalloyed by ambition, such military genius, such an indomitable will, and such a capacity for handling the largest armies ?

For four years and more this man of continuous Luck, across a rugged continent, in the face of armies of men as brave as his own, commanded by generals of extraordinary ability, performed every function of strategy in grand War, which Jomini attributes to Napoleon and his greatest marshals, and Napier to Wellington. Whether Grant could have conducted a successful retreat cannot be known. He was never defeated.

Grant has been severely criticized for the waste of life. War is not created for the purpose of saving life, but by a noble spending of blood to save the Commonwealth. The great end which he achieved would have been cheaply gained, at double the expense.

But we are not to forget the circumstances under which the conduct of the last great campaign was committed to him. For four years the heroic and patient Army of the Potomac had squandered blood and treasure without measure, and had gained not a step. With generals many, excellently skilled in logistics, skillful in everything but success, they fought and retreated; they dug, they waded, they advanced and retreated. They went down to Richmond and looked upon it, and came back to defend Washington.

Their victories were fruitless. Antietam was ably fought, but weakly followed up. Gettysburg, with hideous slaughter, checked Lee's Northward advance and sent him back— but unpursued, undestroyed, though he waited three or four days, helpless, cooped·up.

The Army of the Potomac needed a general who knew how to employ their splendid bravery, their all-enduring pluck. They had danced long enough; they had led off— changed partners—chasséd—they had gone into campaigns with slow and solemn music, but returned with quick-steps. They seemed desirous of making war so as not to exasperate the South.

Do not men know that nothing spends life faster than unfighting war? Disease is more deadly than the bullet. In all the war, but one out of every forty-two that died were slain by the bullet, and one out of every thirteen by disease. Six million men passed through the hospitals during the war; over three million with malarial diseases.

It seemed doubtful whether the Government was putting down rebellion, or whether Lee was putting down the Government. An eminent critic says : " The fire and passion, downright earnestness and self-abandon that the South threw into the struggle at the outset and maintained for two full years, had, it must be admitted, so far impaired the morale of the Union forces, that while courage was nowhere wanting, self-confidence had been seriously diminished. This was especially true of the devoted and decimated Army of the Potomac, whose commanders, after the first battle of Bull Run, always appeared to be afraid of exasperating the enemy. Driving Lee to extremities was the one thing that they were all loth to do. They would fight to the last drop of blood to defend Washington, to hold their own, to preserve the Union, but to corner the enemy, to drive him to desperation, to make him shed the last drop of his own blood, was the one thing they would not do, and no amount of urging could make them do it. It was this *arrière pensée* that held the hand of McClellan and of Meade after Antietam and Gettysburg. Both of these engagements were victories for the Army of the Potomac, and both were robbed of their fruits by a lurking fear of the lion at bay. 'They are *shooing* the enemy out of Maryland,' said Lincoln, with his peculiar aptness and homeliness."

When Grant came to the Army of the Potomac, he reversed the methods of all who preceded him. Braver soldiers never were, nor more valiant commanders; but the generals had not learned the art of fighting with deadly intent. Peace is very good for peace, but war is organized rage. It means destruction or it means nothing.

At the Battle of the Wilderness, Grant stripped his commissary train of its guards to fill a gap in the line of battle. When expostulated with for exposing his army to the loss of all its provisions, his reply was:

" *When this army is whipped, it will not want any provisions.*"

All summer, all the autumn, all the winter, all the spring, and early summer again, he hammered Lee, with blow on blow, until, at Appomattox, the great, but not greatest, Southern general went to the ground.

Grant was a great fighter, but not a fighter only.

His mind took in the whole field of war— as wide and complex as any that ever Napoleon knew. He combined in his plans the operations of three armies, and for the first time in the war, the whole of the Union forces were acting in concert.

He had the patience of Fate, and the force of Thor. If he neglected the rules of war, as at Vicksburg, it was to make better rules, for those who were strong enough to employ them.

Counsellors gave him materials. He formed his own plans. Abhorring show, simple in manner, gentle in his intercourse, modest and even diffident in regard to his own personality, he seems to have been the only man in camp who was ignorant of his own greatness. Never was a commander etter served, never were subordinates more magnanimously treated. The fame of his generals was as dear to him as his own. Those who might have been expected to be his rivals were his bosom friends. While there were envies and jealousies among minor officers, the great names, Grant, Thomas, Sherman, Sheridan, give to history a new instance of a great friendship between great warriors.

# Eulogy on Grant

Some future day a Napier will picture the final drama: the breaking up of Lee's right wing at Five Forks; Lee's retreat; Grant's grim, relentless pursuit; Sheridan, like a raging lion, heading off the fleeing armies, that were wearied, worn, decimated, conquered; and, at the end, the modesty of the victorious general; the delicacy with which he treated his beaten foe; the humanity of the terms given to the men—sent away with food, and horses for their farms; all this will form a picture of *War* and of *Peace*.

Grant never forgot that the South was part of his country. The moment that the South lay panting and helpless upon the ground, he carried himself with magnanimous and sympathetic consideration. After the fall of Richmond he quietly returned to Washington, without entering the conquered capital.

When Johnston surrendered to Sherman upon terms not agreeable to Lincoln, Stanton, like a roaring lion fearing to lose its prey, sent Grant to overrule the victor. Grant loved Sherman, and was unwilling to enter his camp lest he should seem to snatch from him the glory of his illustrious campaign. From a near town he enabled Sherman to reconstruct his terms, and accept General Johnston's surrender.

When Lincoln was dead, Vice-President Johnson became President; a man well fitted for carrying on a fight, but not skilled in peace. With a morbid sense of justice, he determined that the leaders of rebellion should be made to suffer as examples; as if the death of all the first-born, the desolation of every Southern home, the impoverished condition and bankruptcy of every citizen were not example enough! He ordered Lee to be arrested. Grant refused. When Johnson would have employed the army to effect his purposes, Grant, with quick but noble rebellion, refused obedience to his superior, and, arranging to take from his hands all military control, repressed the President's wild temper and savage purpose of a dishonouring justice.

Having brought the long and disastrous war to a close, in his own heart Grant would have chosen to have rested upon his laurels, and lived a retired military life. It was not to be permitted. He was called to the Presidency by universal acclaim, and it fell to him to conduct a campaign of Reconstruction even more burdensome than the war.

It would seem impossible to combine in one, eminent civil and military genius. To a certain extent they have elements in common.

# Eulogy on Grant

But the predominant element in war is organized *Force;* of civil government, *Influence.*
Statesmanship is less brilliant than generalship,
but requires a different and a higher moral and
intellectual genius. God is frugal in creating
great men—men great enough to hold in eminence the elements of a great general and of
a great ruler. Washington was eminent in
statesmanship and a daring warrior—but then
he was not a great general: or, if he was, he
had no opportunity to develop the fact.

Alexander was a mere brutal fighter.

Cæsar as Emperor differed from Cæsar as
General only as a sword sheathed differs from
a sword unsheathed.

Frederick the Great was simply a military
ruler.

Napoleon came near to combine the two
elements in the earlier period of his career,
but the genius of force gradually weakened
that sense of right and justice on which statesmanship must rest.

Grant had in him the elements of great
statesmanship; but neither his education, nor
his training, nor the desperate necessities of
war, gave it a fair chance of development in a
condition of things which bewildered the
wisest statesmen.

The tangled skein of affairs would have tasked a Cavour or a Bismarck. The Period of Reconstruction is yet too near our war-inflamed eyes to be philosophically judged.

First came the disbanding of the army. That was so easily done that the world has never done justice to the marvel. The soldiers of three great armies dropped their arms at the word of command, dissolved their organizations, and disappeared. To-day the mightiest force on earth—to-morrow they were not! As a summer storm darkens the whole heavens, shakes the ground with its thunder, and empties its quiver of lightning, and is gone in an hour, as if it had never been, so was it with both armies. Neither in the South nor in the North was there a cabal of officers, nor any affray of soldiers—for every soldier was yet more a citizen.

In this resumption of citizen life, Grant, accompanied by his most brilliant generals, led the way. He hated war, its very insignia, and in foreign lands refused to witness military pageants. He had had enough of war. He loved peace.

When advanced to the Presidency, three vital questions were to be solved.

1. The status of the four million emancipated slaves.

2.  The adjustment of the political relations of the dislocated States.

3.  The restraint and control of that Gulf Stream of finance which threatened to wash out the foundations of honest industry, and which brought to the Nation more moral mischief than had the whole war itself. We are in peril from golden quicksands yet.

Grant was eminently wise upon this question. His Greenback veto saved the country from a vitiated and corrupting circulation.

The exaltation of the domestic Africans to immediate citizenship was the most audacious act of faith that ever was witnessed.

Their fidelity to the duties of bondage was most Christian. In all the war, knowing that their emancipation was to be gained or lost, there was never an insurrection, nor a recorded instance of cruelty or insubordination. This came not from cowardice; for when, in the later periods of the war, they were enlisted and drilled, they made soldiers so brave as to extort admiration and praise from prejudice itself. They deserved their liberty for their good conduct.

But were they prepared for citizenship? The safety of our civil economy rests upon the intelligence of the citizen. But the slaves in mass were greatly ignorant.

## Lectures and Orations

It was a political necessity to arm them with the ballot as a means of self-defense.

In many of the Southern States a probationary state would have been wiser, but in others it would have remanded the freedmen to substantial bondage at the hands of the whites.

In this grand department of statesmanship President Grant accepted the views of the most eminent Republicans: Stanton, Chase, Sumner, Thad. Stevens, Fessenden, Sherman, Garfield, Conkling, Evarts, and of all the great leaders.

In the readjustment of the political relations of the South he was wise, generous, and magnanimous. Not a line in letter, speech or message can be found that would wound the self-respect of Southern citizens.

When the dangerous heresy of a Greenback currency had gained political power, and Congress was disposed to open the flood-gates of a rotten currency, his veto, an act of courage, turned back the deluge and saved the land from a whole generation of mischief. Had he done but this one thing, he would have deserved well of History.

The respects in which he fell below the line of sound statesmanship—and these are not a few—are to be attributed to the influence of ad-

visers whom he had taken into his confidence.
Such was his loyalty to friendship that it must
be set down as a fault—a fault rarely found
among public men.

Many springs of mischief were opened which
still flow. When it was proposed to nominate
Grant for a third term, the real objections to
the movement among wise and dispassionate
men was not so much against Grant as against
the staff which would come in with him.

On the whole, if one considers the intrinsic
difficulty of the questions belonging to his administration, the stormy days of politics and
parties during his eight years, it must be admitted that the country owes to his unselfish
disposition, to his general wisdom, to his unsullied integrity, if not the meed of wisest yet
the reputation of one who, preëminent in war,
was eminent in administration, more perhaps
by the wisdom of a noble nature than by that
intelligence which is bred only by experience.
Imperious counsellors and corrupt parasites
dimmed the light of his political administration.

We turn from Grant's public life to his un-
restful private life. After a return from a tour
of the world, during which he met on all hands
a distinguished reception, he ventured upon

the dangerous road of speculation. The desire of large wealth was deep-seated in Grant's soul. His early experience of poverty had probably taken away from it all romance. Had wealth been sought by a legitimate production of real property, he would have added one more laurel to his career. But, with childlike simplicity of ignorance, he committed all he had to the wild chances of legalized gambling. But a few days before the humiliating crash came, he believed himself to be worth three millions of dollars ! What service had been rendered for it ? What equivalent of industry, skill, productiveness, distribution or convenience ? None. Did he never think that this golden robe, with which he designed to clothe his declining years, was woven of air, was in its nature unsubstantial, and not reputable ? His success was a gorgeous bubble, reflecting on its brilliant surface all the hues of heaven, but which grew thinner as it swelled larger. A touch dispelled the illusion, and left him poor.

It is a significant proof of the impression produced upon the public mind of the essential honour of his mind, and of the simplicity of his ignorance of practical business, that the whole Nation condoned his folly, and believed in his intentional honesty. But the iron had entered his soul. That which all the hardships of war, and the wearing anxieties of public administration could not do, the shame and bitterness of this great Bankruptcy achieved.

The resisting forces of his body gave way. A disease in ambush sprang forth and carried him captive. Patiently he sat in the region and shadow of death. A mild heroism of gentleness and patience hovered about him. The iron will that had upheld him in all the vicissitudes of war, still in a gracious guise sustained his lingering hours.

His household love, never tarnished, never abated, now roused him to one last heroic achievement—to provide for the future of his family. No longer were there golden hopes for himself. The vision of wealth had vanished. But love took its place, and under weakness, pain and anguish, he wrought out a history of his remarkable career. A kindly hand administered the trust. It has amply secured his loved household from want.

When the last lines were written, he lay back upon his couch and breathed out his great soul to God, whom he had worshipped unostentatiously after the manner of his fathers.

A man he was without vices, with an

absolute hatred of lies, and an ineradicable love of truth, of a perfect loyalty to friendship, neither envious of others nor selfish for himself. With a zeal for the public good, unfeigned, he has left to memory only such weaknesses as connect him with humanity, and such virtues as will rank him among heroes.

The tidings of his death, long expected, gave a shock to the whole world. Governments, rulers, eminent statesmen and scholars from all civilized nations gave sincere tokens of sympathy. For the hour, sympathy rolled as a wave over all our own land. It closed the last furrow of war, it extinguished the last prejudice, it effaced the last vestige of hatred —and cursed be the hand that shall bring them back!

Confederate Johnston and Buckner on one side, Federal Sherman and Sheridan upon the other of his bier, he has come to his tomb a silent symbol that Liberty had conquered Slavery; Patriotism, Rebellion; and Peace, War.

He rests in peace. No drum or cannon shall disturb him more.

Sleep, Hero, until another trumpet shall shake the heavens and the earth. Then come forth to glory in immortality!

# IX

## ABRAHAM LINCOLN [1]

THERE is no historic figure more noble than that of the Jewish lawgiver. After so many thousand years the figure of Moses is not diminished, but stands up against the background of early days distinct and individual as if he had lived but yesterday. There is scarcely another event in history more touching than his death. He had borne the great burdens of state for forty years, shaped the Jews to a nation, filled out their civil and religious polity, administered their laws, guided their steps, or dealt with them in all their journeyings in the wilderness; had mourned in their punishment, kept step with

[1] At Plymouth Church, Brooklyn, Sunday morning, April 23, 1865. Mr. Beecher, returning with the steamer's guests from the Fort Sumter flag raising of April 14th, met in New York the fatal news of the President's assassination. He went direct to Peekskill, and the following Sunday gave this discourse. His text was *Deuteronomy* xxxiv. 1–5,—the brief account of how Moses was led by the Lord to the top of Mount Pisgah, whence he viewed the promised land of Canaan, before his death there in the mountain.

their march, and led them in wars until the end of their labours drew nigh. The last stage was reached. Jordan, only, lay between them and the " promised land."

The Promised Land! O what yearnings had heaved his breast for that divinely fore-shadowed place! He had dreamed of it by night, and mused by day; it was holy and endeared as God's favoured spot. It was to be the cradle of an illustrious history. All his long, laborious, and now weary life, he had aimed at this as the consummation of every desire, the reward of every toil and pain. Then came the word of the Lord to him: " Thou mayest not go over. Get thee up into the mountain; look upon it; and die!"

From that silent summit the hoary leader gazed to the north, to the south, to the west with hungry eyes. The dim outlines rose up. The hazy recesses spoke of quiet valleys between hills. With eager longing, with sad resignation, he looked upon the promised land. It was now to him a forbidden land. This was but a moment's anguish; he forgot all his personal wants, and drank in the vision of his people's home. His work was done. There lay God's promise, fulfilled. There was the seat of coming Jerusalem; there the city of Judah's King; the sphere of judges and prophets; the Mount of sorrow and salvation; the nest whence were to fly blessings innumerable to all mankind. Joy chased sadness from every feature, and the prophet laid him down, and died.

Again a great leader of the people has passed through toil, sorrow, battle, and war, and come near to the promised land of peace, into which he might not pass over. Who shall recount our martyr's sufferings for this people! Since the November of 1860, his horizon has been black with storms. By day and by night he trod a way of danger and darkness. On his shoulders rested a government dearer to him than his own life. At its integrity millions of men at home were striking; upon it foreign eyes lowered. It stood like a lone island in a sea full of storms; and every tide and wave seemed eager to devour it. Upon thousands of hearts great sorrows and anxieties have rested, but not on one, such, and in such measure, as upon that simple, truthful, noble soul, our faithful and sainted Lincoln. Never rising to the enthusiasm of more impassioned natures in hours of hope, and never sinking with the mercurial in hours of defeat to the depths of despondency, he held on with un-

# Lectures and Orations

movable patience and fortitude, putting caution against hope that it might not be prema-
ture, and hope against caution that it might
not yield to dread and danger. He wrestled
ceaselessly, through four black and dreadful
purgatorial years, wherein God was cleansing
the sins of His people as by fire.

At last the watcher beheld the gray dawn
for the country. The mountains began to
give forth their forms from out of the darkness; and the East came rushing towards us
with arms full of joy for all our sorrows. Then
it was for him to be glad exceedingly, that had
sorrowed immeasurably. Peace could bring
to no other heart such joy, such rest, such
honour, such trust, such gratitude. But he
looked upon it as Moses looked upon the
promised land.

Then the wail of a nation proclaimed that
he had gone from among us.

Not thine the sorrow, but ours, sainted
soul! Thou hast indeed entered into the
promised land, while we are yet on the march.
To us remain the rocking of the deep, the
storm upon the land, days of duty and nights
of watching; but thou art sphered high above
all darkness and fear, beyond all sorrow and
weariness. Rest, O weary heart! Rejoice

exceedingly, thou that hast enough suffered! Thou hast beheld Him who invisibly led thee in this great wilderness. Thou standest among the elect. Around thee are the royal men that have ennobled human life in every age. Kingly art thou, with glory on thy brow as a diadem. And joy is upon thee forevermore. Over all this land, over all the little cloud of years that now from thine infinite horizon moves back as a speck, thou art lifted up as high as a star is above the clouds, that hide us but never reach it. In the goodly company of Mount Zion thou shalt find that rest which thou hast sorrowing sought here in vain ; and thy name, an everlasting name in heaven, shall flourish in fragrance and beauty as long as men shall last upon the earth, or hearts remain, to revere truth, fidelity, and goodness.

Never did two such orbs of experience meet in one hemisphere, as the joy and the sorrow of the same week in this land. The joy of final victory was as sudden as if no man had expected it, and as entrancing as if it had fallen a sphere from heaven. It rose up over sobriety, and swept business from its moorings, and ran down through the land in irresistible course. Men embraced each other in brotherhood that were strangers in the flesh. They sang, or prayed, or, deeper yet, many could only think thanksgiving and weep gladness. That peace was sure ; that our government was firmer than ever ; that the land was cleansed of plague ; that the ages were opening to our footsteps, and we were to begin a march of blessings ; that blood was staunched, and scowling enmities were sinking like storms beneath the horizon ; that the dear fatherland, nothing lost, much gained, was to rise up in unexampled honour among the nations of the earth,—these thoughts, and that undistinguishable throng of fancies, and hopes, and desires, and yearnings, that filled the soul with tremblings like the heated air of midsummer days,— all these kindled up such a surge of joy as no words may describe.

In one hour, under the blow of a single bereavement, joy lay without a pulse, without a gleam, or breath. A sorrow came that swept through the land as huge storms sweep through the forest and field, rolling thunder along the sky, dishevelling the flowers, daunting every singer in thicket or forest, and pouring blackness and darkness across the land and upon the mountains. Did ever so many hearts, in so brief a time, touch two such boundless feelings ? It was the uttermost of joy ; it was the uttermost of sorrow ;—noon and midnight without a space between !

The blow brought not a sharp pang. It was so terrible that at first it stunned sensibility. Citizens were like men awakened at midnight by an earthquake, and bewildered to find everything that they were accustomed to trust wavering and falling. The very earth was no longer solid. The first feeling was the least. Men waited to get straight to feel. They wandered in the streets as if groping after some impending dread, or undeveloped sorrow, or some one to tell them what ailed them. They met each other as if each would ask the other, " Am I awake, or do I dream ? " There was a piteous helplessness. Strong men bowed down and wept. Other and common griefs belonged to some one in chief; this belonged to all. It was each and every man's. Every virtuous household in the land felt as if its first-born were gone. Men were bereaved, and walked for days as if a corpse lay unburied in their dwellings. There was nothing else to think of. They could speak of nothing but that ; and yet, of that they could speak only falteringly. All business was laid aside. Pleasure forgot to smile. The great city for nearly a week ceased to roar. The huge

Leviathan lay down and was still. Even avarice stood still, and greed was strangely moved to generous sympathy and universal sorrow. Rear to his name monuments, found charitable institutions, and write his name above their lintels; but no monument will ever equal the universal, spontaneous, and sublime sorrow that in a moment swept down lines and parties, and covered up animosities, and in an hour brought a divided people into unity of grief and indivisible fellowship of anguish.

For myself, I cannot yet command that quietness of spirit needed for a just and temperate delineation of a man whom goodness has made great. Leaving that, if it please God, to some other occasion, I pass to some considerations aside from the martyr-President's character which may be fit for this hour's instruction.

And first, let us not mourn that his departure was so sudden, nor fill our imagination with horror at its method. Men, long eluding and evading sorrow, when at last they are overtaken by it seem enchanted and seek to make their sorrow sorrowful to the very uttermost, and to bring out every drop of suffering which they possibly can. This is not Christian, though it may be natural. When good men pray for deliverance from sudden death, it is only that they may not be plunged without preparation, all disrobed, into the presence of their Judge. When one is ready to depart suddenness of death is a blessing. It is a painful sight to see a tree overthrown by a tornado, wrenched from its foundations, and broken down like a weed; but it is yet more painful to see a vast and venerable tree lingering with vain strife against decay, which age and infirmity have marked for destruction. The process by which strength wastes, and the mind is obscured, and the tabernacle is taken down, is humiliating and painful; and it is good and grand when a man departs to his rest from out of the midst of duty, full-armed and strong, with pulse beating time. For such a one to go suddenly, if he be prepared to go, is but to terminate a most noble life in its most noble manner. Mark the words of the Master:

" Let your loins be girded about, and your lights burning; and ye yourselves like unto men that wait for their lord, when he will return from the wedding; that when he cometh and knocketh, they may open unto him immediately. Blessed are those servants whom the Lord when He cometh shall find watching."

Not they that go in a stupor, but they that go with all their powers about them, and wide-awake, to meet their Master, as to a wedding, are blessed. He died watching. He died with his armour on. In the midst of hours of labour, in the very heart of patriotic consultations, just returned from camps and counsels, he was stricken down. No fever dried his blood. No slow waste consumed him. All at once, in full strength and manhood, with his girdle tight about him, he departed; and walks with God.

Nor was the manner of his death more shocking, if we divest it of the malignity of the motives which caused it. The mere instrument itself is not one that we should shrink from contemplating. Have not thousands of soldiers fallen on the field of battle by the bullets of the enemy? Is being killed in battle counted to be a dreadful mode of dying? It was as if he had died in battle. Do not all soldiers that must fall ask to depart in the hour of battle and of victory? He went in the hour of victory.

There has not been a poor drummer-boy in all this war that has fallen for whom the great heart of Lincoln would not have bled; there has not been one private soldier, without note or name, slain among thousands and hid in the pit among hundreds, without even the memorial of a separate burial, for whom the President would not have wept. He was a man from the common people who never forgot his kind. And now that he who might not bear the march, and the toil, and the battle with these humble citizens has been called to die by the bullet, as they were, do you not feel that there was a peculiar fitness to his nature and life that he should in death be joined with them in a final common experience to whom he had been joined in all his sympathies?

For myself, when any event is susceptible of a higher and nobler garnishing, I know not what that disposition is that should seek to drag it down to the depths of gloom, and write it all over with the scrawls of horror or fear. I let the light of nobler thoughts fall upon his departure, and bless God that there is some argument of consolation in the matter and manner of his going, as there was in the matter and manner of his staying.

Then, again, this blow was but the expiring rebellion. As a miniature gives all the form and features of its subject, so, epitomized in this foul act, we find the whole nature and disposition of slavery. It begins in a wanton

destruction of all human rights, and in a desecration of all the sanctities of heart and home;
and it is the universal enemy of mankind, and
of God, who made man. It can be maintained
only at the sacrifice of every right moral feeling in its abettors and upholders. I deride
him who points me to any one bred amid
slavery, believing in it, and willingly practic-
ing it, and tells me that he is a man. I shall
find saints in perdition sooner than I shall find
true manhood under the influences of so accursed a system as this. It is a two-edged
sword, cutting both ways, violently destroying
manhood in the oppressed, and insidiously
destroying manhood in the oppressor. The
problem is solved, the demonstration is completed in our land. Slavery wastes its victims,
and it destroys the masters. It kills public
morality, and the possibility of it. It corrupts
manhood in its very centre and elements.
Communities in which it exists are not to be
trusted. They are rotten. Nor can you find
timber grown in this accursed soil of iniquity
that is fit to build our Ship of State, or lay the
foundation of our households. The patriotism
that grows up under this blight, when put to
proof, is selfish and brittle; and he that leans
upon it shall be pierced. The honour that

grows up in the midst of slavery is not honour,
but a bastard quality that usurps the place of
its better, only to disgrace the name.    And, as
long as there is conscience, or reason, or
Christianity, the honour that slavery begets
will be a byword and a hissing.    The whole
moral nature of men reared to familiarity and
connivance with slavery is death-smitten.    The
needless rebellion; the treachery of its leaders
to oaths and solemn trusts; their violation of
the commonest principles of fidelity, sitting in
senates, in councils, in places of public confidence only to betray and to destroy; the long,
general, and unparalleled cruelty to prisoners,
without provocation, and utterly without excuse; the unreasoning malignity and fierceness,—these all mark the symptoms of that
disease of slavery, which is a deadly poison to
soul and body.

I do not say that there are not single natures, here and there, scattered through the
vast wilderness which is covered with this
poisonous vine, who escaped the poison.
There are; but they are not to be found
among the men that believe in it, and that
have been moulded by it.    They are the exceptions.    Slavery is itself barbarity.    That
nation which cherishes it is barbarous; and

no outside tinsel or glitter can redeem it from the charge of barbarism. And it was fit that its expiring blow should be such as to take away from men the last forbearance, the last pity, and fire the soul with an invincible determination that the breeding-ground of such mischiefs and monsters shall be utterly and forever destroyed.

We needed not that he should put on paper that he believed in slavery, who, with treason, with murder, with cruelty infernal, hovered around that majestic man to destroy his life. He was himself but the long sting with which slavery struck at liberty; and he carried the poison that belonged to slavery. As long as this Nation lasts, it will never be forgotten that we have had one martyred President—never! Never, while time lasts, while heaven lasts, while hell rocks and groans, will it be forgotten that slavery, by its minions, slew him, and in slaying him made manifest its whole nature and tendency.

But another thing for us to remember is that this blow was aimed at the life of the Government and of the Nation. Lincoln was slain; America was meant. The man was cast down; the Government was smitten at. It was the President who was killed. It was national life, breathing freedom and meaning beneficence, that was sought. He, the man of Illinois, the private man, divested of robes and the insignia of authority, representing nothing but his personal self, might have been hated; but that would not have called forth the murderer's blow. It was because he stood in the place of Government, representing government and a government that represented right and liberty, that he was singled out.

This, then, is a crime against universal government. It is not a blow at the foundations of our Government, more than at the foundations of the English government, of the French government, of every compacted and well-organized government. It was a crime against mankind. The whole world will repudiate and stigmatize it as a deed without a shade of redeeming light. For this was not the oppressed, goaded to extremity, turning on his oppressor. Not even the shadow of a cloud of wrong has rested on the South, and they know it right well.

In a council held in the city of Charleston, just preceding the attack on Fort Sumter, two commissioners were appointed to go to Washington; one on the part of the army from Fort Sumter, and one on the part of the

Confederates. The lieutenant that was designated to go for us said it seemed to him that it would be of little use for him to go, as his opinion was immovably fixed in favour of maintaining the government in whose service he was employed. Then Governor Pickens took him aside, detaining for an hour and a half the railroad train that was to convey them on their errand. He opened to him the whole plan and secrets of the Southern conspiracy, and said to him, distinctly and repeatedly (for it was needful, he said, to lay aside disguises), that the South had never been wronged, and that all their pretenses of grievance in the matter of tariffs, or anything else, were invalid. "But," said he, " we must carry the people with us ; and we allege these things, as all statesmen do many things they do not believe, because they are the only instruments by which the people can be managed." He then and there declared that it had simply come to this : that the two sections of country were so antagonistic in ideas and policies that they could not live together ; that it was foreordained that, on account of differences in ideas and policies, Northern and Southern men must keep apart. This is testimony which was given by one of the leaders in the

Rebellion, and which will probably, ere long, be given under hand and seal to the public. So the South has never had wrongs visited upon it except by that which was inherent in it.

This was not, then, the avenging hand of one goaded by tyranny. It was not a despot turned on by his victim. It was the venomous hatred of liberty wielded by an avowed advocate of slavery. And, though there may have been cases of murder in which there were shades of palliation, yet this murder was without provocation, without temptation, without reason, sprung from the fury of a heart cankered to all that was just and good, and corrupted by all that was wicked and foul.

The blow, however, has signally failed. The cause is not stricken; it is strengthened. This Nation has dissolved—but in tears only. It stands, four-square, more solid, to-day, than any pyramid in Egypt. This people are neither wasted, nor daunted, nor disordered. Men hate slavery and love liberty with stronger hate and love to-day than ever before. The Government is not weakened, it is made stronger. How naturally and easily were the ranks closed! Another stepped forward, in the hour that the one fell, to take his place and his mantle; and I utter my trust that he will be found a man true to every instinct of liberty; true to the whole trust that is reposed in him; vigilant of the Constitution; careful of the laws; wise for liberty in that he himself, through his life, has known what it was to suffer from the stings of slavery, and to prize liberty from bitter personal experiences.

Where could the head of government in any monarchy be smitten down by the hand of an assassin, and the funds not quiver nor fall one-half of one per cent.? After a long period of national disturbance, after four years of drastic war, after tremendous drafts on the resources of the country, in the height and top of our burdens, the heart of this people is such that now, when the head of government is stricken down, the public funds do not waver, but stand as the granite ribs in our mountains. Republican institutions have been vindicated in this experience as they never were before; and the whole history of the last four years, rounded up by this cruel stroke, seems now in the providence of God to have been clothed with an illustration, with a sympathy, with an aptness, and with a significance, such as we never could have expected or imagined. God, I think, has said, by the voice of this event, to all nations of the earth, " Republican liberty, based upon true Christianity, is firm as the foundation of the globe."

Even he who now sleeps has, by this event, been clothed with new influence. Dead, he speaks to men who now willingly hear what before they refused to listen to. Now, his simple and weighty words will be gathered like those of Washington, and your children and your children's children shall be taught to ponder the simplicity and deep wisdom of utterances which, in their time, passed, in the party heat, as idle words. Men will receive a new impulse of patriotism for his sake, and will guard with zeal the whole country which he loved so well; I swear you, on the altar of his memory, to be more faithful to the country for which he has perished. Men will, as they follow his hearse, swear a new hatred to that slavery against which he warred, and which in vanquishing him has made him a martyr and a conqueror; I swear you, by the memory of this martyr, to hate slavery with an unappeasable hatred. Men will admire and imitate his unmoved firmness, his inflexible conscience for the right, and yet his gentleness, as tender as a woman's, his moderation of spirit, which not all the heat of party could inflame, nor all the jars and disturbances of this country shake out of its place ; I swear you to an emulation of his justice, his moderation and his mercy.

You I can comfort; but how can I speak to that twilight million to whom his name was as the name of an angel of God? There will be wailing in places which no ministers shall be able to reach. When, in hovel and in cot, in wood and in wilderness, in the field throughout the South, the dusky children, who looked upon him as that Moses whom God sent before them to lead them out of the land of bondage, learn that he has fallen, who shall comfort them? Oh, Thou Shepherd of Israel, that didst comfort Thy people of old, to Thy care we commit the helpless, the long-wronged, and grieved!

And now the martyr is moving in triumphal march, mightier than when alive.[1] The Nation rises up at every stage of his coming. Cities and States are his pallbearers, and the cannon beats the hours with solemn progression. Dead—dead—dead—he yet speaketh! Is Washington dead? Is Hampden dead? Is

[1] The funeral journey, conveying Lincoln's body from Washington to Illinois, was fourteen days in progress. Assassinated on April 14th, he was buried on May 4, 1865.

# Abraham Lincoln

David dead? Is any man dead that ever was fit to live? Disenthralled of flesh, and risen to the unobstructed sphere where passion never comes, he begins his illimitable work. His life now is grafted upon the Infinite, and will be fruitful as no earthly life can be. Pass on, thou that hast overcome! Your sorrows, O people, are his peace! Your bells, and bands, and muffled drums sound triumph in his ear. Wail and weep here; God makes it echo joy and triumph there. Pass on, thou victor!

Four years ago, O Illinois, we took from your midst an untried man, and from among the people; we return him to you a mighty conqueror. Not thine any more, but the Nation's; not ours, but the world's. Give him place, ye prairies! In the midst of this great Continent his dust shall rest, a sacred treasure to myriads who shall make pilgrimage to that shrine to kindle anew their zeal and patriotism. Ye winds, that move over the mighty places of the West, chant his requiem! Ye people, behold a martyr, whose blood, as so many articulate words, pleads for fidelity, for law, for liberty!

# Appendix

## PATRIOTISM ABOVE PARTY

[IN 1884, the public were intent upon two especial reforms,—one, of the inequalities and inefficiencies of the Tariff, by which the Republican party in its long lease of power was thought to have been corrupted; the other, of the methods of appointment to positions in the Civil Service, wherein naturally the party in power were held to be the offenders in the wide-spread official demoralization of that time. Many Republicans were urgent for these reforms, and of course their political opponents, the Democrats, were vociferous for them.

Thus, both parties became in their platforms committed to the same lines of promised betterment, and the probability or improbability of reform was to be looked for in their Presidential candidates. The Republican candidate was James G. Blaine; the Democratic candidate, Grover Cleveland. Mr. Blaine's public career did not satisfy the reforming element of his own party, while Mr. Cleveland's course commended him to

# Patriotism Above Party

the Democrats (except of the New York Tammany type) and to many of the Republicans, who supported—and elected him.

Among the Independent Republicans was Mr. Beecher, who wrote and spoke for Cleveland, and, when charged with treason to the Republican party, made the following campaign speech in Brooklyn, in October, 1884. The newspaper report, with its interpolations of what the audience thought about it, is allowed to stand. It is an example of Mr. Beecher's aptitude in popular appeal.]

I confess, at the risk of the imputation of some immodesty, that my appearance here to-night to antagonize the organized action of the Republican party, is itself a fact of the most significant character. Before many of you were born I was rocking the cradle of the Republican party. [*Applause.*] I fought its early battles when it was in an apparently hopeless minority. I advocated its cause, speaking day and night, at the risk of my health and of my life itself [*applause*] when Frémont was our first notable candidate. When Mr. Lincoln [*cheers*] became our candidate I gave all I had of time, strength, influence, and persuasion, and when his election was ascertained and efforts were made to intimidate the North and to prevent his being chaired, I went up and down through this country stiffening the backs of willow-backed patriots. [*Applause and laughter.*] I faced mobs, I preached day and night in my own church, to hold the North up to its own rights and interests. When the war broke out I sent to it the only boy I had big enough to hold a musket [*applause*], and it greatly grieved my oldest child, a daughter, that she was not a boy. [*Laughter and applause.*] As the war went on my contribution could not be much, but such as it was I gave it—I gave it as a mother gives her breast to her child. [*Renewed applause.*]

And when, seeking some rest from exhausting cares and labours, I went abroad, I did not suffer the grass to grow under my feet, but in the face of royalty and aristocracy and of great wealth in England I upheld the justice and the rectitude of the cause for which we were all striving. [*Great applause.*] And at every canvass from that day to this I have not held back health, strength or influence. Why, then, is it that I am now opposed to the organized movement of the Republican party? That is a significant question. For, gentlemen, I have never fed on official pap. [*Laughter and applause.*] I have never asked a favour for myself, nor could one be given me. I would not take a seat in the Senate of the United States, even if I could get it, and I fear that I am too good a man to get it. [*Great laughter.*] Pardon me some little vanity when I say that I regard the platform of Plymouth Church as unspeakably

higher than the Presidency of these United States—
for me, not for others. [*Renewed laughter and applause.*]

I am now opposing the party whose cradle I
rocked, because I do not mean to be a pall-bearer
to carry the coffin of that party to the grave.
[*Applause.*] Gentlemen, the Republican party is
on its way to destruction, unless you turn the
switch and run it on a side track. [*Laughter.*]
And by all my love of my country—and it is next
to my love of my God—by all my pride in the
past—I feel bound to do whatever God will inspire
me to do to stop the ruinous progress of the Republican party and to save it. [*Applause.*]

It behooves you, therefore, not to make mere
amusement of the work of this evening. I speak to
you as to a jury. The case before you is not that
of some trembling culprit, or some wronged citizen
seeking redress. It is your whole country that is
before you to-night, whose cause I am to plead—to
plead as if life or death hung on the issues. [*Applause.*] I am in dead earnest. It is very natural
that men working through a political party should
by and by come to look upon all events in the community in their relation to party welfare and party
success. But I, who have had nothing to do with
parties, except as moral instruments, naturally look
upon their movements and purposes from the moral
standpoint. What are they attempting to do for
this great people? What does their success mean?

# Appendix

How does it stand alongside the intelligence, the morality, the true religion of this people, alongside that patriotism which rests its feet on morality, but whose head stands in the spirituality which connects man with God? [*Great applause.*] I study public affairs from the moral and religious standpoint, and that which is offensive to God may I never live to see the day when it may be acceptable to me and to my countrymen. [*Renewed applause.*]

Looking forward, as the pilot looks, what are our perils? The war is over. The great questions that agitated the community are past. You can't bring them back. There are, however, two great dangers that betide our Government. One is the danger that comes from the corrupt use of wealth; the other, that which comes from the corruption of too-long-held power. [*Great applause.*] It is a common proverb, "An honest man can bear watching—a dishonest man needs it." [*Laughter.*] This is just as true of politics as of common procedure. This is the age of enterprise, of production, of commerce—of money. All the world is a great buzzing factory, and the making of money stands, of all things, the most conspicuous to the visual sense. Russia, Austria and France failed in their greatest recent wars and enterprises because those countries were honeycombed with official corruption. We are in danger from the same cause. The heavens rain gold on us; every drop of our summer showers is worth more than a dollar to us. The annual increase of wages among the labouring people is over $700,000,000, and they are taxed $1,200,000 a year ! Yet we have an organization calling itself a " protection to the working man ! " It is a great scheme of taxation that rolls $4,000,000,-000 a year into the reservoirs at Washington, and $100,000,000 stagnates there uselessly, besides exhaling an atmosphere of corruption. [*Applause.*]

It would be strange indeed if some of this golden water in the mill-dam of Washington were not employed to grind out votes to-day for the " old Republican party." It is ! One of the greatest dangers of our day is bribery. Voters are bribed. Thousands of men carry their hands open for their dollar or their two dollars, and put their vote in for that price and then wipe their smudged faces and go home and say their regular prayers. [*Laughter.*] Men who wish to go to the Legislature know how it is. "Money makes the mare go"—and the legislator ! [*Laughter.*] It is scarcely possible for a man to go to the United States Senate unless he or his friends have the *quid pro quo.* Now and then there is a Sumner, but they don't grow on every bush. [*Laughter.*] The Senators from Kansas, from Nevada, from California, are not suffered to go to Washington at their own expenses; or, if at their own expenses, they take care of those that send them there. [*Laughter.*] Our very courts often receive upon their benches judges placed there by the influence of gain—not for themselves, for I believe them as a body to be just men, but their friends use inducements by which they are sent to the bench.

To-day it is sought to buy a candidate into the Presidential chair with money. I have been credibly informed that between one and two million dollars have been rolled west to gild the State of Ohio, and a like stream is pouring into Indiana. My early life was spent in Indiana, my elder children were born there, and, in my heart, a Hoosier is, as it were, a brother to me, and anything that is good for Indiana pleases me. When, therefore, in the last conflict of 1880 word came that Dorsey had succeeded in carrying that State for the Republican party, I felt so grateful that I told Mr. Murphy that I would be glad to go to a public dinner in honour of Mr. Dorsey, and I went—innocent as I was! [*Great laughter.*] I think that confidence in my fellow men and generosity have been the occasion of more of my trips and downfalls than any vices or any other offenses. [*Renewed laughter and applause.*]

When I see Mr. Dudley abandoning his duties in Washington and distributing money with an unshamed hand—willing to acknowledge that he is doing it—I say that the thing is coming very nearly home to me, and that one great danger in the near future is that we shall have a Government that will be honeycombed with pecuniary corruption. What a rush there is for gold! How impatient are men become of homely industry—how eager for unearned properties—how eager for speculation, which is, in the main, an attempt to cheat the devil. [*Laughter.*] Who can count the reputable thieves that have stolen trust funds and run off with bonds committed to their custody—presidents, cashiers, directors, clerks, agents; this one a leading deacon, that one a Sunday-school superintendent; all of them Christians! [*Great laughter.*] Oh, if Christ were here, would He not again begin to drive out from the temple of our liberty the money-changers and those who sold doves and oxen and asses—and men!

Now, under such circumstances, I ask you, which man will be the most likely to meet and resist this cankerous tendency—Mr. Blaine or Mr. Cleveland? [*Tremendous enthusiasm and cheers for Cleveland.*] What would Mr. Blaine do for the reform? He would not allow Mr. Dudley to forsake the Pension Bureau in order to teach the people to worship the golden calf.—Would he? [*Laughter.*] He would not allow Congress to donate lands to railroads.—Would he? [*Renewed laughter.*] He would seize the Pacific Railroads by the throat and help Thurman and Edmunds to drag them to settlement.—Wouldn't he? [*Great laughter.*]

What is the tone of moral sense of people who, when a body of men are anxious to redeem the

# Appendix

Government from corruption, or to prevent it, call them dudes and Pharisees?—as if to seek to stem the tide of corruption was to say, "I am holier than thou; I am a Pharisee." Who was the Pharisee? In the earlier day he was the Puritan of the Jews. The Pharisees were the men that in the Babylonish captivity undertook to keep their own people from idolatry, and to hold them to the worship of Jehovah. They were the Puritans of the Orient, as the English were the Puritans of the Occident. It was the Puritan that gave liberty to old England, and it was the Puritan that brought liberty to New England and laid the foundations of the institutions on which we stand. So the Pharisees were the Puritans, and in that sense I am a Pharisee, thank God! [*Tremendous applause.*] Whether I am a dude, I don't know. [*Uproarious laughter and applause.*] But if the sluices are to be kept open, and jobbery permitted to run riot, no more fitting selection could be made for the Presidency than James G. Blaine. [*Applause.*]

I am a personal friend of Mr. Blaine. [*Laughter.*] For twelve years I have watched him, anxious that he should be the right man—that he is not. For more than ten years I have been afraid of him. I have been challenged by a Brooklyn paper to give an account of an interview I had with Mr. Blaine at the Fifth Avenue Hotel. I have only this to say about it. I don't think Mr. Joy exists any longer [*laughter*] as a respondent. If he does,

there is something more to be said. But after I
spoke at the Cooper Union in advocacy of Mr.
Garfield's election, nearly four years ago [*cheers*],
I received a request from Mr. Blaine to meet him
at the Fifth Avenue Hotel. Taking my eldest son
with me, I went over. Mr. Blaine asked me if I
had seen the newspaper called *Truth*. I said,
"No." "Let me read it to you," said he. He
read me, I should think, two columns. I replied,
"That paper has one-third truth and two-thirds
lies." [*Laughter.*] "Now," said I, "I will tell
you just what the truth was." I then narrated to
him my interview with Mr. Joy. I was struck,
after narrating it, that he didn't fly into anger—
that he didn't peremptorily and with the indignation
of an honest man deny it. Without quoting his
words, this was their substance : "Why, this can't
be. I don't remember that I ever had any trans-
actions in that direction. I don't think that I had
any bonds or anything of that kind at that time.
Why, it is not probable ; Mr. Joy—he couldn't have
said any such thing as that."

By that time I was touched a little. I said to
him : "Mr. Blaine, where then did I get the story ?
Did I make it up, or did Mr. Joy tell it to me ?"
"Oh," he said, "no, of course, but then Mr. Joy
is my best friend. He introduced my name into
the convention at Chicago, and advocated my
nomination." "Yes, sir," said I, "and that is
the most damning circumstance about it. [*Great*

# Appendix

*applause.*] For, sir, when they found that you were the man that these monopolists and consolidated railroads wanted, they attempted to put you where you could do the most good." [*Laughter and applause.*] After some further discussion—for both of us were polite on the outside and extremely indignant on the inside—we parted. This is the interview that the *Brooklyn Times* challenged me, once and again, to relate. May that paper make the most of it. [*Great applause.*]

I met Mr. Blaine once after that, and had some conversation with him. Going out from the Adams Express office and walking down the street, he said : "What do you think of the Cabinet that Garfield is to form?" My reply was, "Well, I don't meddle with such things much. The only thing I know is who ought to be Secretary of State." "Who?" said he. Said I, "James G. Blaine." "Do you think so? I wish you would write that to Mr. Garfield." I replied that I did not like to meddle with such matters, but I would think it over. I did not write.

You may ask me how I should have made such a suggestion to Mr. Blaine, with the opinion that I held of him. I reasoned in this way : I knew Mr. Garfield was under great obligations to Mr. Blaine, and that beyond all question he would have the proffer of some chair in the Cabinet. I thought : It won't do for him to go to the Interior Department ; there are too many temptations. It will certainly

# Patriotism Above Party

never do for him to be put in the Treasury.
[*Laughter.*] Although he is a good letter-writer
he would not accept the Post-Office. In my simplicity I thought that the next thing to extradition
and emigration would be to put him in the chair of
the Secretary of State. So simple was I! [*Laughter.*] And therefore I thought, as he must go into
the Cabinet, that was the place where he could do
the least harm.

Now, the other great danger to which our Government is exposed is to be found in organizing all the
officers of the Government and drilling them into a
compact body, not for the people, but for the party
that happens to be in the ascendency. There are
between 80,000 and 100,000 officers under the Federal Government. In the year 1900 there will be
multitudes more. To meet this danger, Civil Service
Reform has been instituted. You will remember it
began with a few, and was hardly thought worthy
of notice. When it was urged, politicians began
to resist it. Little by little, the sober sense of the
common people saw its necessity and it received a
tentative organization. Finally it became a system,
with its laws.

Rotation in office is bad for the Government, because the change of minor officers with every change
of administration leaves the Government continually
in the condition of being served by raw men. No
mercantile establishment, no foundry or ship-
building concern would turn off its expert labourers

and take on green hands, but that is what our Government has been doing every time the party has changed, thus bringing into the service inexperienced and unfit men. It is bad also because it holds up not patriotism as the motive of activity, but this bribe of an office. These are dangerous to the Government, corrupting to the people, and they forebode by and by an oligarchy that can determine almost every election by the people. [*Applause.*]

Has Mr. Blaine ever done anything for Civil Service Reform? From under his roof, where dwells one of the most brilliant and acute writers in the great school of women writers,[1] there issued the most caustic and ridiculing series of letters on the whole matter of reform and reformers in this respect. If I mistake not, it was composed under his roof, on his tables, and under his eye, and—unrebuked. Was there ever any testimony from him except this —a mild praise of Garfield as believing in Civil Service Reform and an acceptance of the platform of the Republican party that indorsed it? Is that the man to *enforce* Civil Service Reform?

Now, on the other hand, is there one of these elements of danger which we have to fear at the hands of Mr. Cleveland? [*Cheers and applause.*] He is a lawyer of repute, known for the sound judgment and the great industry which he brings to his cases. He began public life as a sheriff. He has

[1] " Gail Hamilton " was the nom de plume of Mary Abigail Dodge.

been the subject of ridicule in that matter, and from quarters where I did not expect it, I believe last night—perhaps the night before—in this place. It has been laughed at that he charged for 860 days in a year of service, as if there were 860 days, and yet the fools that are laughing do not know that more than half the work of the sheriff is done by deputies, and every deputy's service is counted by the day. This is understood by legislatures and by courts. The very man in that county who is now up for Congress returned 1,100 days' service in the 365, and doubtless very properly, too. He is a Republican candidate. They laugh because Sheriff Cleveland charged twenty-five cents for newspapers. Mr. Blaine would have charged $200. But this man Cleveland has no idea of dishonesty. He does not know what his privileges were ! You will bear in mind that when Marcy was Governor of New York and had to travel the State, he charged, I think, three shillings or fifty cents for mending his pantaloons. He that is faithful in little will also be faithful in great things. [*Laughter*.]

Now, I want a man that won't take one single, solitary penny but simply what belongs to him. In these buncombe days, when men don't count a dollar worth anything, it is good to find the original simplicity of the old-fashioned men who served the public. But Judge Davis sneered at Cleveland as a sheriff because he himself personally superintended

# Appendix

the execution of one whom the law had doomed
to death. He—a judge—an able judge—a judge
whose memory will go down to posterity as having
convicted that arch criminal Tweed [*applause*], so
far forgot himself as to say that Mr. Tanner was a
good candidate for sheriff, and I say " Amen " to
that. I shall vote for him. [*Applause.*] But he
also said—this is the offensive part—that he would
not vote for him if he thought that in executing the
law he would personally superintend the execution
of a culprit. A judge from the bench saying to
the young men who gathered here that a law and
statute of the commonwealth was honoured in having a sworn officer refuse to execute it ! [*Cries of
" Shame ! shame !" and hisses.*]

Now, Judge Davis would never have said that
deliberately. It is one of those little excursions
that public speakers sometimes make. [*Laughter.*]
From the Shrievalty Mr. Cleveland was exalted to
the Mayoralty—if it be an exaltation, and in some
cities it is, but we will wait until after the election
in New York and see. [*Laughter.*] As such he
won a good repute and was honoured by the whole
bulk of the citizens of Buffalo. Then, as a rebuke
to the managers of the Republican party, he was
exalted to the position of Governor of the State of
New York. [*Applause.*] Nor has there been any
sort of chance to make any effectual criticism on his
administration since he has been Governor of this
imperial State. [*Applause.*] In this position,

simple as a child, sincere ˜as a saint [*applause*], with
broad common sense and very uncommon honesty
[*applause*], a true and enthusiastic member of the
Democratic party [*applause*], but putting the
whole State and the whole country higher than the
party, he has been steadily and patiently perform-
ing the duties of his office, while Mr. Blaine has
been imitating the pot-house politicians in the ward
elections. As they go from house to house and
grog-shop to grog-shop, so Blaine goes from town
to town, hat in hand, a national mendicant
soliciting votes, as medicants solicit doles of
charity; dishonouring the example of all Presidential candidates we have ever had up to this hour,
except the solitary instance of Mr. Whitelaw Reid's
great predecessor, Horace Greeley! Blaine has ex-
hibited his person throughout New York State and
throughout Ohio, throughout Indiana and Michigan,
and is coming back soon to upset everything in
Brooklyn and New York. [*Laughter.*] During
this extraordinary and not honourable exodus of
Blaine, Grover Cleveland remained at home steadfast to duty. He attended to the duties of his office
and let the country employ its own best judgment
as to whether he should go higher. [*Applause.*]

One reason why Mr. Cleveland is not acceptable
to some of his own party is that while he is an
honest Democrat he is not a partisan, but a patriot.
[*Applause.*] Let me attend to some of the objections. If our country needs a man of sterling

honesty and integrity on account of the temptations of money, Cleveland is the man ! [*Applause.*] If our Government is to be free from the dangers of a complex financial combination that can determine for any party in power very nearly the whole future, Cleveland is the man. [*Great applause.*] Do you know that when he came into the Governor's chair he never turned out a man that his predecessor Cornell had put in power but one? Cornell had turned out a one-armed soldier as a messenger and put in a stalwart working-man. Cleveland put out the stalwart working-man and put back the one-armed soldier. [*Applause.*] One-half of his staff to-day are Republicans. That's the man for Washington ! [*Applause.*]

But this is almost the one argument I hear on every hand—"I don't like Blaine. He was not my choice, but then, he is the regular nominee of our party." Well, I should like to know what sort of a party man you are that can stand by and see your party degraded and damaged, but stick to it and not put forward one single, solitary effort to save it. [*Applause.*] And yet the party is not like the man that fell among the thieves—though the thieves are after it. [*Laughter.*] Here are the men who see the danger. And the priest saw that the poor fellow wasn't a priest and he went past ; and the Levite (as it has been said) saw that he had been robbed already and he went past. [*Great laughter.*] But if you are a faithful Republican, the command is as if it came from the lips of God, "See that the party suffers no detriment," and no greater detriment could come than an unworthy head given to it.

Why, according to your logic, you must vote for whomsoever the convention gives you. If the convention had given you Tweed, every mother's son of you would have had to drop your tail between your legs and vote for Tweed. The logic of this is infamous, and the man who urges such an excuse as that, if he has a decent wife, ought not to go home for forty-eight hours, until he had bathed and cleansed himself. Suppose you were the trustee of an academy or school and you knew that the man whom the trustees had elected was utterly untrustworthy, you would say, "I belong to the Board of Trustees, and I must go as they go, and I will send my boy to the school whatever this man may be." You would not do it anywhere else, I tell you, except where the murrain of a blighted politics had fallen upon you.

Well, they say, "We don't wish to leave the party." We don't wish to have you. We want you to stay in it and become Independent Republicans. [*Applause.*] Who are Independent Republicans? They are the men who seek to raise the party to the higher ground. They are the men who hailed the rising sun and don't want to see the setting sun go down in clouds and darkness. They are the men who watch the temptations of the day,

its dangers, and set themselves to maintain the
honour of party and country. These men "don't
want to leave the party." Suppose you were
travelling in a stage-coach and plunged headlong
down an embankment into mud and morass, and
the driver cries, "Come, out with you, out with
you all, and help me put it back again," and every
mother's son of you should say, "No; we are not
going to leave this coach."

I should say, if I were driver, "Get the coach
out of the mud, and then get in again or go afoot!"

To elect Mr. Blaine under all the conditions, under all the charges and imputations, and in the
light of all his history, is to say to every unprincipled man on this continent, "No matter what
your life has been, if you get a regular nomination,
you are going to be in the Presidential chair." I
shall attend to what men say about teaching our
young people to vote for the morality of Mr. Cleveland before I close; but I return the question to
you: "Will you teach your children that lying is
a safe thing, a mere blemish, a foible?" I tell you
that truth is the one cohesive element that holds
society together. [*Applause.*] I tell you that
truth is that bond which creates trust between man
and man, and to put a man smouched with lies in
the Presidential chair is to teach all our young men
that lying is a foible and not a sin.

But they say again, "We are not going to join
the Democratic party. We have fought all our

life long against it. We are not going to change now." Well, we have not joined the Democrats except for one end, and that is to keep out a bad man and put in a good one. [*Applause.*] Suppose they do take the Government. Do you undertake to say that there are no good Democrats? and that, too, when you see that it was the best men of the Democratic party that put forward Cleveland against other and very strong candidates, because he was an honest and good man? [*Applause.*] I tell you that either party alone will not produce as good results as the best men of the two parties working together for a common purpose. [*Applause.*] If the Democrats, long out of power, do well, I want them to retain administrative power. [*Applause.*] If, with four years' power, they prove themselves incompetent we will whirl them out as the dust is whirled from the threshing-floor. [*Applause.*] I defy them to do much worse than I think Blaine will. [*Applause.*]

But there is another thing for you to carry in mind and to interpret, and that is, what Independent Republicanism means. It is, as yet, an undeveloped third party. It will hold the balance between the two parties. It will be a voice in every election, saying: "If you present worthy men we'll help you. If you present unworthy men, we'll defeat you." [*Applause.*] So degraded has been the political conscience, however, that the Republican leaders pour contempt on the very idea

# Appendix

that there can be uncorrupted politics, and they ridicule the conception that the Independent Republicans have got any cleaner hands and any higher motives than anybody else. Nevertheless they will find out, if not in this election then in the next, for we have not come together to be easily dissolved. The men who are forming the backbone, the ribs, the hands, and the feet of the Independent Republicans are the men who propose to stand by this work right through the years. We are the men who have such a pride in our Government and in our country that we decree our lives to the maintenance of its purity, its dignity, and its grandeur.

The great ends for which the Republican party was formed have been grandly accomplished. But this very accomplishment lays upon us new duties growing out of the past. It is not for Republicans to sit down like misers and count over our gains.

Our first endeavour was to secure free speech : we gained it.

The right to attack slavery and put bounds to its spread ; the right to put the government into the hands of men who love liberty rather than slavery. We elected Lincoln ; we put him into the Presidential chair.

We exploded the doctrine of the sovereignty of States, though we affirm the limited doctrine of State Rights. The vicious heresy of the right of secession—we put our foot on that serpent, and it will never squirm again. For the maintenance of the war we freely gave our substance and that which is above all treasure, our sons.

It is not to be forgotten that, in this renowned war, we were gallantly helped by the noblest element in the Democratic party. Our most notable generals sprung from that party.

We have liberated the slave and have wiped the shame and disgrace of slavery from off our escutcheon.

We have passed through the clouded and difficult work of Reconstruction, and the States are knit together and are working in good neighbourhood and harmony. We have well-nigh paid the six thousand million debt entailed by the war, we have brought back the currency to a specie basis, and driven the greenback heresy to the wilderness.

All these questions have been settled so thoroughly that they have drifted beyond the horizon and out of party discussions. The old Republican and the old Democratic parties are now so nearly agreed that their two platforms are almost identical. Platforms no longer mean principles—policies that run down to the foundations of government. Platforms to-day are mere policies for to-day, and the Republican and the Democratic platforms might almost be swapped without either party perceiving the difference.

God calls us now to turn our face to the future.

# Appendix

What is the business of to-day? What are the great questions of the near future?

First and most immediate, is Civil Service Reform, which in his sleeve Blaine laughs at; next, the limitations of great monopolies; the dangerous power of aggregated capital; a lawful control of the combined railroads; a vigorous sympathy and rigorous watchfulness of the rights of the common people, who gain their livelihood by labour; freedom of commerce, as the last link in the slowly-forged chain of freedom; liberty of thought, of conscience, of speech, of motion and action, and liberty of commerce—the liberty of men to come and go, for traffic, over the wide earth.

The education of all the people, at public expense, by the Federal government where it cannot be adequately done by the States.

The rights of labour as against combined capital, and the defense of the individual as against the despotism of corporate bodies. The safety of an American citizen at home and abroad; peace with all the world, but war if we must. No Socialism, no Communism, no Nihilism.

These are the questions of the hour. The Independent Republicans will seek to bring the Old Republican party to generous action upon them.

We are working for the future—not counting the deeds of the past. But it is said Cleveland cannot control the Democratic party; he will be controlled by them. He will oust all the officeholders, and put in Bayard, Thurman, Hurd, Carlisle, Morrison, Lamar, and such like. Well, would that not be a better cabinet than Dorsey, Elkins, Filley, and a whole brood more; would you not like to see Jay Gould sitting in the Treasury? [*Laughter.*] One man shakes his head and says, "Things are so mixed, I shall not vote again." That is like the soldier in the fierce battle who stands with his gun and won't fire because he does not know whom he will hit. We don't want any cowards. It is a man's sworn duty to this Government to vote.

If you vote for Blaine, you vote for corruption. If you vote for St. John,[1] you vote into the air. If you vote for Butler, you vote into the mud. If you vote for Cleveland [*cheers*], you vote for an honest man. [*Loud cheers.*] I don't wish to be one-sided. I don't deny to Mr. Blaine many excellencies as a private citizen. He is kindly and impulsive. He will do his best to serve a friend, if it does not interfere with his personal aim. He loves to render personal services to those who approach him. Such qualities attach men to him. They excite enthusiasm in unreflective people who do not stop to consider whether he is a good leader. Mr. Blaine's personal and social attractions are such and so many that one cannot but think that Providence designed him to stay at home.

But another point:—in all the history of poli-

---

[1] The Prohibitionist candidate.

tics no lies so cruel, so base, so atrocious, have ever been set in motion. The air is murky with shameless stories of Mr. Cleveland's private life. To our sorrow and shame we find these cocatrice's eggs, brooded and hatched by rash and credulous clergymen. They could not go to Mr. Cleveland with honest inquiry, so they opened their ears to the harlot and the drunkard. They have sought by hint, innuendo, irresponsible slander, to poison the faith of holy men, of innocent women, and they have sought to make backbiting a virtue, and to change the sanctuary into a salacious whispering gallery. Is it for our sins, or for a trial of our faith, that God has permitted the plagues of Egypt to revisit us? The land swarms with vermin, frogs slime our bread troughs, and lice crawl about our chambers.

Do timid ministers ever reflect that the guilt of a vice or a crime measures the guilt of him who charges them falsely? Slander takes on the guilt of crime alleged. True religion does not creep through twilight passages, but is open, frank, rejoicing not in iniquity, but rejoicing in the truth, hoping all things. These vespertilian saints, whose soft bat's wings bear them from house to house, and from town to town, in the service of Baal, the god of flies and lies, will one day creep into the holes and clefts of rocks and hide themselves.

My honoured and beloved wife, quite unbeknown to me, cut many cuttings from the newspapers, some

of which—all of which—were in respect to the life
of Governor Cleveland in Albany.   She sent them to
him, with a letter that will not be published, but
that would be a gem in English literature if it were
published.  [*Applause.*]   As swiftly as the mail
could return she received a letter from Governor
Cleveland, which I have had about two or three
weeks, which he means to be private, and marked
private.   But such a complexion has the canvass
taken that I telegraphed to him two nights ago to
ask him if he would allow me to use my discretion
in regard to that letter.   His reply was: "Certainly; if it is your judgment."   [Mr. Beecher
then produced the letter, which he read as follows:]

"MY DEAR MRS. BEECHER:
      "Your letter, as you may well suppose, has
affected me deeply.   What shall I say to one who
writes so like my mother?   I say so like my mother,
but I do not altogether mean that, for she died in
the belief that her son was true and noble, as she
knew he was dutiful and kind.   I am shocked and
dumfounded by the clippings from the newspapers
that you sent me, because it purports to give what
a man actually knows, and not a mere report, as the
other four or five lies do, which I have read or
heard, about my life in Albany.   I have never seen
in Albany a woman whom I have had any reason to
suspect was in any way bad.   I don't know where any
such woman lives in Albany.   I have never been in
any house in Albany except the Executive Mansion,
the Executive Chamber, the First Orange Club
House—twice at receptions given to me and on, I

think, two other occasions—and the residences of perhaps fifteen or twenty of the best citizens, to dine.

"Of course I have been to church. There never was a man who has worked harder or more hours in a day. Almost all my time has been spent in the Executive Chamber, and I hardly think there have been twenty nights in the year and nine months I have lived in Albany—unless I was out of town—that I have left my work earlier than midnight to find my bed at the Mansion. I am at a loss to know how it is that such terrible, wicked, and utterly baseless lies can be invented. [*Applause and cheers*, during which Mr. Beecher placidly remarked, "Do not spend your breath; there is a good deal more coming."] The contemptible creatures who coin and pass these things appear to think that the affair which I have not denied makes me defenseless against any and all slanderers.

"As to my outward life in Buffalo, the manifestation of confidence and attachment which was tendered me there by all citizens must be proof that I have not lived a disgraceful life in that city. And as to my life in Albany, all statements that tend to show that it has been other than laborious and perfectly correct are utterly and in every shape untrue. [*Applause.*] I do not wonder that your good husband is perplexed. I honestly think I desire his good opinion more than any aid he is disposed to render me. I do not want him to think any better of me than I deserve, nor to be deceived. Cannot I manage to see him and to tell him what I cannot write? I shall be in New York Wednesday and Thursday morning, I suppose, of next week. Thursday afternoon and evening I shall

spend in Brooklyn. Having written this much it
occurs to me that such a long letter to you is un-
necessary and unexpected. It is the most I have
ever written on the subject referred to, and I beg
you to forgive me if your kind and touching letter
has led me into impropriety.

" Yours, very sincerely,<br>
" GROVER CLEVELAND."

When in the gloomy night of my own suffering,
I sounded every depth of sorrow, I vowed that if
God would bring the day star of hope, I would
never suffer brother, friend, or neighbour to go un-
friended, should a like serpent seek to crush him.
That oath I will regard now. Because I know the
bitterness of venomous lies, I will stand against infamous lies that seek to sting to death an upright
man and magistrate. Men counsel me to prudence
lest I stir again my own griefs. No! I will not
be prudent. If I refuse to interpose a shield of
well-placed confidence between Governor Cleveland
and the swarm of liars that nuzzle in the mud, or
sling arrows from ambush, may my tongue cleave
to the roof of my mouth, and my right hand forget
its cunning. I will imitate the noble example set
me by Plymouth Church in the day of my own
calamity. They were not ashamed of my bonds.
They stood by me with God-sent loyalty. It was
a heroic deed. They have set my duty before me,
and I will imitate their example.

# THE HERBERT SPENCER DINNER

[IN 1855 Herbert Spencer began his Evolutionary
publications with " Principles of Psychology," and
in 1860 he issued the prospectus of his vast " System of Synthetic Philosophy," extending the principle of Evolution to most developments of nature
and humanity. In 1882 he made a brief visit to
America, where his books had received warm welcome, and just before he returned to England a
complimentary dinner was given him, the gathering
comprising men of eminence, mostly in science.
Among them, however, was Mr. Beecher, who had
been foremost among clergymen in utilizing
Spencer's expositions of the development theory,
which had been, at first vaguely and later more
clearly, his own inspiration. He was to speak,
but at the end of the evening—nearly midnight—
when all were tired and ready to depart. Evolution was not then accepted as it is now, but was
under suspicion as an enemy of religion and the
Bible, and most pious folk regarded Mr. Beecher
as very "loose" and "dangerous." But he was
never afraid to speak his mind, and on that evening he spoke it clearly.

" I shall never," wrote Dr. William A. Ham-
mond, "forget the effect which his ringing words

produced upon that audience, composed as it was mainly of hard-headed men who were not accustomed to be swayed by their emotions. They rose to their feet, waved their table-napkins, and shouted themselves hoarse, not because they all approved of the views which he then revealed to them, but because of the astounding courage, the wonderful regard for the truth as he understood it, and the almost superhuman honesty by which he must have been actuated."

As in the Blaine-Cleveland speech, the report is given as it was taken down at the time.]

The old New England churches used to have two ministers ; one was considered as a doctor of theology, and the other a revivalist and pastor. The doctor has had his day, and you now have the revivalist. [*Laughter.*] Paul complained that Alexander the coppersmith did him much harm. Mr. Spencer has done immense harm. I don't believe that there is an active, thoughtful minister in the United States that has not been put in a peck of troubles, and a great deal more than that, by the intrusion of Mr. Spencer's views, and the comparison of them with the old views. I cannot for the life of me reconcile his notions with those of St. Augustine. I can't get along with Calvin and Spencer both. [*Laughter.*] Sometimes one of them is uppermost, and sometimes the other, and I have often been disposed to let them fight it out themselves, and not take any hand in the scrape. [*Laughter.*] It is to be borne in mind that when a man is driving a team of fractious horses that are just all that he can manage anyhow, he is not in a state of mind to discuss questions with his wife by his side, who is undertaking to bring up delicate domestic matters. [*Laughter.*] A man who has a bald-headed deacon watching everything that he does, or a gold-spectacled lawyer—not a fat one [*looking at Mr. Bristow*], but a long, lean, lank one [*looking at Mr. Evarts, amid great laughter*] —can't afford to talk Spencerism from the pulpit ; he has got to take care of himself first, and he must therefore not be expected to come in like an equi-noctial storm ; he will rather come in like a drizzle ; he will descend as the dew. [*Laughter.*]

But one thing is very certain—Mr. Spencer is coming. Nay, he has come; he has come to stay. Mr. Spencer may have dyspepsia, but his books have no dyspepsia. [*Applause.*] They like the climate, and they are working their way very steadily, without any regard to those dietetic or nervous or nervine considerations which he has been kind enough to propose to us here to-night. Those books can work day and night everywhere, all over the continent, and never grow any thinner.

By the by, when he speaks about our being so industrious, he speaks like an insular gentleman. You have very little to do in England. You have

# The Herbert Spencer Dinner

but about three hundred miles diameter one way and eight hundred the other. We have got this whole continent to take care of. [*Laughter.*] We have to get up early and work late in order to take care of it. We are an ambitious people, and we have learned from astronomers that they are five hours ahead of us every day in England, and we have to work with all our might to make up those five hours. [*Laughter.*] We don't intend to be surpassed by the old people on the other side. We young people on this side intend to do as well as they have done and a little better.

Now let me say, with a little more approach to sobriety [*laughter*], what I think about the doctrines of Mr. Spencer's philosophy. Not all his admirers or debtors or disciples need adopt his conclusions fully. We may deem his base line to be correct, and yet not be surprised if here and there parts of his vast field should need to be resurveyed. But, speaking in general terms, I think that the doctrine of Evolution and its relations to the work of Mr. Spencer—which takes in that, but a great deal more besides—to speak in plain language, is going to revolutionize theology from one end to the other [*applause*], and it is going to make good walking where we have had very muddy walking hitherto ; it is going to bridge over rivers which we have had to wade. There are many points in which the theology of the past did well enough for the past, but does not any more answer the reason-

# Appendix

able questions and the moral considerations that are
brought to bear upon it in our day. [*Applause.*]
We are to bear in mind in regard to the Scriptures,
the great source of instruction on the part of the
organized religions of the Christian world, that we
have there what we all agree in.   Some points
have already been made in regard to it.   Paul
speaks of his idea of what the whole drift of Christianity was.   It was a system *to make men.*   That
is what it was.   He said, To some He gave apostles
and prophets, and evangelists and teachers, for the
perfecting of the saints, that they may become perfect men in Christ, or upon the model of Christ
Jesus.   The New Testament idea is that religion is
the art of putting men on to an anvil and hammer-
ing them out into perfect manhood.   Now there
is no difference between that tendency in the
Scriptures on that subject and in Mr. Spencer's
work or Mr. Darwin's, or any other of that galaxy
of eminent writers that shine in the East.

Then, on the other hand, taking that for the
ideal, that the whole business of religion is not
merely to insure a man against fire in the other
world, but to create an insurable interest in him
[*laughter*], the business before men is the making
of themselves while they are making also the world
in which they dwell, building up society, bringing
that day when the very wilderness shall bud and
blossom as the rose ; making manhood ethics, in
short, of the building kind.   And in that regard

# The Herbert Spencer Dinner

the morality which is taught in Mr. Spencer's work is entirely in agreement with the great morality that is taught in the sacred Scriptures.

Men forget that the Scripture itself—and it ought to have dawned on the minds of the men who are so afraid it will be destroyed—is itself a proof of Evolution. There is no fact more absolutely patent than that every moral idea from the opening of Genesis, right straight through the period in Judges and down to the New Testament day— every one of the great moral ideas rose like a star, and did not shine like a sun until ages had given it ascension. [*Applause.*] The very conception of the divine nature begins at daylight and goes on to sunrise and to meridian brightness; and all the doctrines of duties and relations in the Old Testament are progressive from the beginning down clear through to the end. The doctrine of immortality was not known in the Old Testament day. Here we have Professor Park, of Andover, and a great many good and godly men in New England, discussing to-day whether a man who don't believe that everybody who dies impenitent will be damned forever and ever—whether he is fit to preach the Gospel; and yet for more than five thousand years there was not a man living on the face of the earth that knew there even was a future. [*Applause.*] We have the implicit declaration in the New Testament that life and immortality were brought to light by Jesus Christ. For more than five thousand years men did not know anything fit to preach, according to the modern notion.

But look at the great question of the origin of men. It is a hypothesis that we are but the prolongation of an inferior animal tribe, and there are many evidences among men that it is so. [*Laughter.*] I can almost trace the very lines on which some men have come down. [*Laughter.*] It is said that we descend from the immortal monkey; but that is not the truth that is taught, as I understand it, in the books. You have got to go a great way further back than that to find your grandfather. Apes came down from the same starting-point with us, working towards bone and muscle, and men came down on the other side, working towards nerve and brain. A great many people are loath to think that such an origin should be hinted at by science, that it should stand even as a hypothesis. I would just as lief have descended from a monkey as from anything else if I had descended far enough. [*Laughter.*] But let men have come from where they will, or how they may have come, one thing is very certain, that the human race began at the bottom and not at the top, or else there is no truth in history or religion; and that the unfolding of the human race has been going on, if not from the absolute animal conditions, yet from the lowest possible savage conditions; and the Jewish legend that men were at the top, and then fell from the top to the bottom, and carried down all their posterity with them, and that God's business has been for eight, ten, twenty thousand years, and how many more I know not, the punishing of men for sins they never committed—well, that has got to go. [*Applause.*] It will not be twenty years before a man will be ashamed to stand up in any intelligent pulpit and mention it. [*Applause.*]

On the other hand, see what light is thrown upon Divine Providence. According to the old theology, one single person was sorted out, an emigrant, and the whole of the divine thought was centred on him and on his posterity, and all the collateral races of every kind were left without a temple, without a book, without a priest, without a Sabbath, without a sacrifice, without an altar, without anything, while he brought up one single family; and what a family! [*Laughter.*] And what bringing up! [*Laughter.*] What a means of grace it was to have had those twelve patriarchs! In modern society those men could not have lived, with the exception, perhaps, of one or two of them; they could not have lived outside of Sing Sing—unless they went into politics. [*Laughter.*] They went down to Egypt and there they were abandoned to slavery for four hundred years. What was done for them? Nothing. They came out of Egypt, and, passing forty years through the wilderness, came into the eastern line of Palestine and took possession, by the sword, of the land,

# Appendix

slaughtering the inhabitants, and for four hundred years there was an interregnum again, until we come down to the time of Samuel, and even after that there is no continuity of organized government. The hiatus between one period and another, the interregnum periods, when you come to put them together, negative the current and conventional conception of the nature of the special tutelary administration of God over a chosen people, relieving them from the operation of the laws of social progress. On the other hand, when you come to look at the actual facts and take the whole human family, they have been steadily and gradually unfolding, some with greater rapidity and some less. Some were more capable of thought than others; some were stronger in hand and tarried by the way to fight; but on the whole the world has been, with unequal speed, advancing from the earliest period down to the present time. This is a great deal more consonant with any rational idea of an overruling Providence and a divine justice than the ideas of the old theologies.

Then comes the question of sin. I am taught by Augustine and Calvin, and all of the mediæval preachers, that there are two sorts of sin: one is " original sin "—I have always been original enough to have my own sin [*laughter*]—but that we are all under conditions of guilt, wrath, and penalty, on account of the transgression of Adam and Eve, nobody knows how many thousand years ago; that the guilt of their inexperience—their transaction in the garden of Eden—ran clear down through the thousands of years, and included every child that was born from that time to this. Now what is the theory that comes on the other hand, on the side of science? It is the theory that man is first an animal pure and simple; that by the breathing of the breath of God into him there is the unfolding gradually of a rational soul, an intellectual capacity, a moral and a spiritual nature; that while he was an animal the exercise of selfishness, of plunder, of combativeness and destructiveness, was the law of his being,—it was not only a necessity, but the act was a virtue; yet by gradual development he has come to the possession of those higher qualities which should rule him. Sin lies in the conflict between animal nature and the dawning of spiritual, moral and intellectual nature. It is the conflict in a man between his upper and lower nature.

If you want to see that taught thoroughly, go to the seventh of Romans and see how Paul argues the matter. He says: "The things I would do, I do not; the things I would not do, I do. So then, it is not I," he says, "but sin that dwelleth in me. I find a law in my members." (He was almost fit to be a minister to Darwin!) "I find a law in my members that compels me to sin, but that I in which my personal identity is, the I that thinks, the I that perceives, that aspires, the flash

# Appendix

of imagination (which he calls faith), the whole
fruition of a great soul that approves the spiritual
law, the manly law—whatever is right, pure, just,
beautiful—I see that, but I am all the time doing
the other. My under man, my physical man, is
fighting against the upper man.''

There isn't a man here but knows that that is so.
Every evening rebukes every morning among the
whole of you. You go out in the morning with inspiration and noble feeling, and say, '' This day I
will cheat nobody,'' and you come back at night
and you have cheated a dozen men. [*Laughter.*]
And so on through the whole scale of conduct.
Great light is thrown, by this truly scientific and
truly spiritual view, on the subject of the nature of
sin. I might go on and show that in many other
ways religious teaching is largely benefited by the
light coming from the great thinkers of the day.

Now men say, Will you abandon revelation?
No. We all believe, who believe in Moses, that
God wrote on stone. I believe that that was not
the first time he wrote on stone. He made a record when he made the granite, and when he made
all the successive strata in the periods of time.
There is a record in geology that is as much a
record of God as the record on paper in human
language. [*Applause.*] They are both true—
where they are true. [*Laughter.*] The record of
matter very often is misinterpreted, and the record
of the letter is often misinterpreted ; and you are to

# The Herbert Spencer Dinner

enlighten yourselves by knowing both of them and interpreting them one by the other.  It is no more a quarrel between science and religion, than a discussion over family matters is a quarrel between the husband and wife; it is simply a thorough adjustment of affairs.  [*Laughter.*]

Gentlemen, we have had a good time here to-night, too much of it, especially for a man like me that can't eat because he has a speech to make. We shall very soon break up.  It is not our privilege to meet Mr. Spencer face to face as we all would be glad to do; I certainly would.  I don't know of a man living, with whom, if I might sit down in the shade of the evening, in quiet, and bring up my crude thought, my vagrant imagination, and avail myself of his superior experience and thought—I know of no man now living with whom I should feel more honoured and more pleased in communing than with him.  It is not in my nature to derive benefit from any mortal soul and forget the obligation.  I feel in my pulse a longing that goes back to the early days, to Homer, and comes down through the whole catalogue of noble writers who have written that which the world thought worth preserving; and every man that comes up in our day, and whose writings fortify me and strengthen me—I would fain carry some tribute of affection to him.  I began to read Mr. Spencer's works more than twenty years ago.  They have been meat and bread to me.  They have helped me through a great many difficulties. I desire to own my obligation personally to him, and to say that if I had the fortune of a millionaire, and I should pour all my gold at his feet, it would be no sort of compensation compared to that which I believe I owe him; for whoever gives me a thought that dispels the darkness that hangs over the most precious secrets of life, whoever gives me confidence in the destiny of my fellow men, whoever gives me a clearer standpoint from which I can look to the great silent One, and hear Him even in half, and believe in Him, not by the tests of physical science, but by moral intuition—whoever gives that power is more to me than even my father and my mother; they gave me an outward and a physical life, but these others emancipate that life from superstition, from fears, and from thralls, and make me a citizen of the universe. [*Applause.*]

May He who holds the storm in His hand be gracious to you, sir; may your voyage across the sea be prosperous and speedy; may you find on the other side all those conditions of health and of comfort which shall enable you to complete the great work, greater than any other man in this age has ever attempted; may you live to hear from this continent and from that other, an unbroken testimony to the service which you have done to humanity; and thus, if you are not outwardly crowned, you wear an invisible crown on your head that will carry comfort to death—and I will greet you beyond !

# Index

# Index

mouthpiece of his time, 158; and Lyman Beecher, 159; sectarianism modified, 163–164; aids in changing view of God, 165–169; since, religion advanced, 170–175; a godly man, light in darkness, 179–180; testified against slavery, 222–223

Choate, Rufus, 199

Chronology, 94

Cicero, 151

Civil liberty of individual, 27–29

Civil Service Reform, 296, 306

Civil War, the, North and South, 242–243; survey of forces in, 244–246; death and disease in, 249–250

Cleveland, Grover, Appendix I, *passim*, 284–311

Common people, Reign of the, Chapter III, 94–127; education of, 62–64, 96–105; intelligence of, affecting science, religion, government, 120–125

Connecticut, 13

Constitution, compromises of, 213

Conversation a realm of oratory, 135

DARWIN, CHARLES, 65, 320

Davis, Judge, 297–298

Death, sudden, 270

Delaware, 14

Democratic party in the War, 242

Demosthenes, 151

Despotism concentres, liberty diffuses, 24

Dorsey, Republican worker, 290, 307

Douglass, Frederick, 221

Drunkenness, social burden, 84–86

Dudley, Pension Commissioner, 290

EDUCATION of common people, 62–64, 96–105

Egypt, education in, 96

Elkins, Senator, 307

Eloquence and Oratory, Chapter IV, 128–156; valuable for spread of learning, knowledge, and right motive, 130, 131; largely ignored by pulpit, platform and bar, 133, 134; requisites—training of whole body for expression of great thoughts, 138–150; examples, 151; compared with books and press, 153; is the living power of man on man, 155

Emancipation in North, 211–213

Emerson, Ralph Waldo, 194, 198

England, 183, 288

Episcopal Church, the, 177–178

Europe an armed camp, 89

Evarts, Wm. M., 314

Everett, Edward, 199

Evolution and the Bible, 317

Excitements classified, 65

# Index

# Index

# Index

# Index

*Printed in the United States of America*